Painting for Pleasure

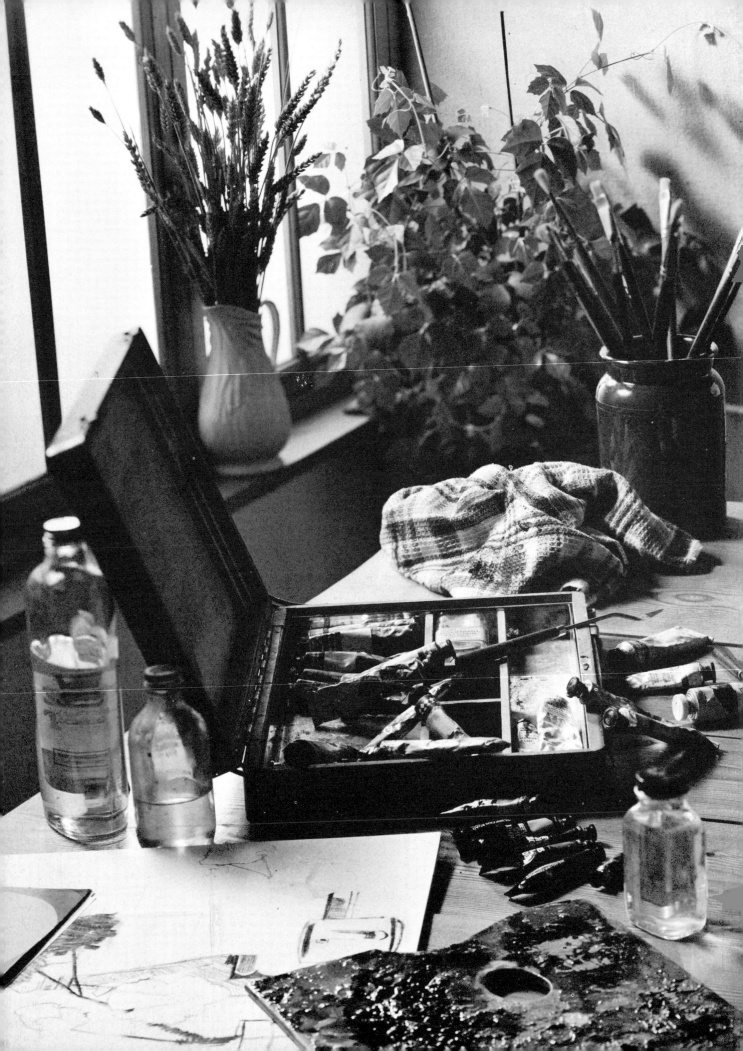

Painting for Pleasure

John FitzMaurice Mills

Hamlyn
London · New York · Sydney · Toronto

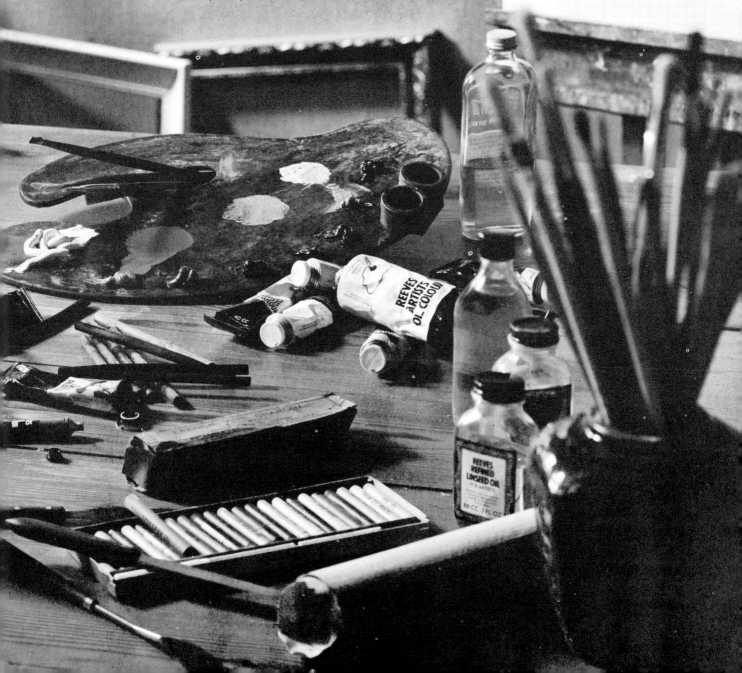

The publishers gratefully
acknowledge the assistance given by
Reeves and Sons Ltd., in supplying
artists' materials shown on the jacket
and used in the colour artwork.

Jacket photograph by John Lee for the
Hamlyn Group.

Published by
The Hamlyn Publishing Group Ltd.,
Astronaut House, Feltham, England
London · New York · Sydney · Toronto
© The Hamlyn Publishing Group Ltd 1977

ISBN 0 600 00230 6

Phototypeset by Tradespools Ltd., Frome, Somerset
Set in 12 on 16pt Monophoto Sabon
Printed in the Canary Islands by Litografia A. Romero
S.A., Santa Cruz de Tenerife (Spain). D. L. TF. 1.193 - 1976

Contents

List of colour plates

The painter and his medium

Man has been painting pictures to order for thousands of years. His inspiration may have been magical, political, religious or a desire of his patron, but not until the twentieth century did the sheer joy of painting burst out as a pursuit for everyman. There is a dormant creative power within nearly everyone that is there to be released. It need not necessarily be a desire for, or have a destiny in, lasting effects, but it is as much a part of a whole person as their eyes, hands and body. Yet for the large majority this release of creative energy and accomplishment remains barred behind a door until it withers and is forgotten.

The door that blocks achievement and pleasure is fear. A false suggestion comes to many that they cannot or will not be able to paint. The fear analysed has no more substance than a shadow that is dispelled by the light. There will be stumbles in the first attempts – what beginnings do not have their trials! In the first moments invisible shackles lock the hands and a mist of personal doubt saps the courage to make those first strokes: it is almost as though there is a physical threat of disaster for the beginner who has the temerity to soil the canvas with the initial marks. This unwarranted fear is best banished by going straight in with a good-sized brush, and as the first strokes are laid down so the demon is vanquished and the adventure has begun.

The act of painting is a joy and experience that brings with it a whole train of emotions, fascination, excitement, achievement. The setting out of colours on the palette, the holding of a brush or painting knife, and the mixing of the colours all serve to generate a sensation of action. The real crescendo starts with the attack on the canvas, panel or paper. There is a heady, intimate and individual sensation in the handling of colour, the feel of the brush passing through it and the delightful realization as an image grows. Perfection of concept, exact likeness, true perspective, proportion, anatomy, are all ends that may or may not be sought, but they need not cramp the first flush of beginning.

To paint is to step outside a routine, a normal day, to glimpse entirely new horizons. It is as though a third eye is suddenly found. Fresh vision brings a widening experience particularly of colour, but with it also a new sensibility to everything that is around; the construction of nature, the relationship of shapes to each other, the subtleties of the play of light and shade. These are the first steps of setting out across the threshold into the vast field of visual infinity. The very mixing of two colours at once underlines this, as innumerable tints and tones spread out across the palette.

The earliest known painters were those who some twenty thousand years ago created wonderful graphic representations of the animals that were so important to them. In caves at Lascaux in France and Altamira in Spain there are displays of pure visual expression. Whether they worked with primitive crushed pigments and medium, or used lumps of charred wood and coloured earths, it is not always certain. But what can be seen is the marvellous sense of freedom in the leaping, galloping deer, cattle and horses that surge across the rock faces. These first artists were not fenced in by fashion, rules and criticism, they drew and coloured with a glorious abandon. The span between their moment and today covers a whole saga of advance in methods, materials, manners, schools and accomplishments. The pinnacles of achievement in this long period have been reached, with technique, with composition, with sophistication. The lessons have been learnt, and the digestion of all these today opens the way to true freedom for painting.

The walls of the tombs in the Valley of the Kings in Egypt are billboards advertising to the next world the prowess of the early pharaohs and their courts. The paintings carried out in variations of watercolour and tempera are allied to cartoons, set out with the exactitude of a cartographer. Disciplined fashions governed the presentation of figures and the relative sizes for the personal importance of the sitters. The compositions may stand static, yet here is man the artist, already sponsored by his patron, beginning the long climb through to the complete understanding of his craft, which we see comes full cycle several thousand years later, once more back to freedom.

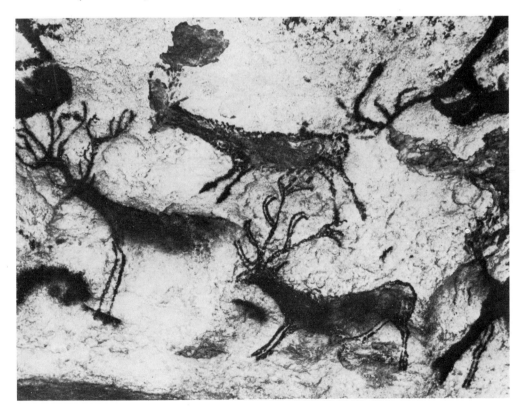

Cave painting at Lascaux, France.

9

The following Mediterranean civilisations added to the knowledge of the use of materials; the sophistication of image grew. The methods used included *buon fresco*, where the painter applied his colours mixed with lime water directly into moist plaster; *tempera*, where in its truest form the pigments are mixed with egg yolk, or in variations with whole egg, egg white, fig milk and a wide variety of vegetable juices and gums; *encaustic*, with the colours bound by wax and where the application was made by using heat; lastly variants of *watercolour*, with the pigments held by natural gums. The colours themselves were drawn from many sources: natural earths, many of which are still current today; plants and mineral salts. Some were permanent, others have altered or perished with time. The ultra-distinct characteristics of national styles – Egyptian, Greek, Byzantine – gradually blurred as predator conquerors sacked not only the countries but also brought back the works of art, where portable, and the artists and craftsmen. In the story of man's rampage, always it seems the victor stole the finest works of art from the vanquished to provide himself with a final accolade or sense of aesthetic power – the Romans and the Goths indulged themselves, and in nearer memory Napoleon and Hitler.

The great classic periods in the art of Greece, and then the Roman Empire, were both preparatory foundations for the real beginning of the arts of the West. To most, this beginning was the outburst of the creative flame in Italy, the Renaissance, the earliest flickerings of which came in the latter part of the fourteenth century when Cimabue and his follower Giotto began to break with the stylism of the Byzantine: painting in its truest form had been born. It was coming through as a visual art that was combining not only power of narrative, but, more important, the aesthetic use of colour and atmosphere. In the next two centuries the great painters of the Renaissance were to understand anatomy, perspective and the use of light and shade. The old mediums, particularly fresco and tempera, were to be exploited to the full. Giotto, Massaccio and Michelangelo transcended the use of pigments from being a laboured method of recording, and gave to their compositions that quality of timelessness which comes with genius. Painting, technically and in content, in two hundred years advanced to maturity: each master brought to it an individual manner, a fresh influence. The ripples from Italy spread out over Europe, carried by travelling painters, or by the purchase of their works. Somewhere in this time a new medium was slowly evolved. Although often attributed as the discovery of the Flemish painters Hubert and Jan Van Eyck, oil painting was a gradual development, as artists used fresh additives with their pigments, as they searched for richer, stronger and brighter effects and colours. Oils mixed with pigments brought a revolution to the palette. The great colourist, Titian, showed the strength of this new medium; glazes brought depths of translucence undreamt of; the colours glowed. The 'will o' the wisp' incandescence of genius jumped national borders and flashed from country to country and period to period: as it faded in Italy, it came to forceful life in the Low Countries, in Spain, in Germany, and in France. Painting was truly on the move, great collections were

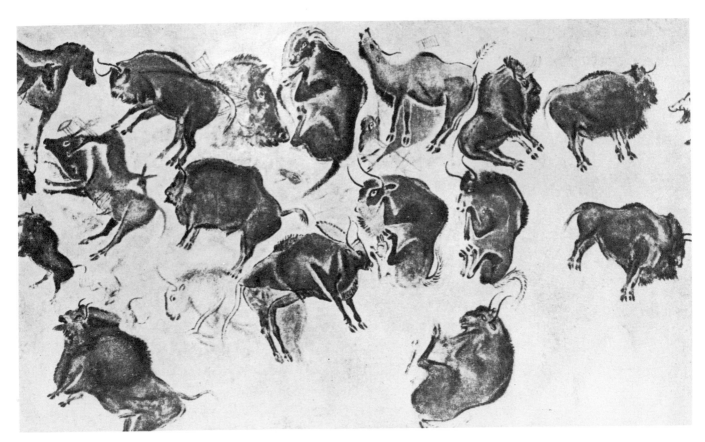

formed, master artists were received as equals in the highest courts. Recognisable schools of painting became more truly defined. The early Flemish masters, the Van Eycks and their contemporaries, left behind superb examples of controlled technique. The Brueghels provided fantasy. From the fabulous Rubens' atelier in Antwerp poured out a vast torrent of paintings, some from the hand of the master, others, part by him and part by a host of assistants who over the years included men of the calibre of Snyders, Teniers, Ostade and Van Dyck.

Cave painting at Altamira, Spain.

To many, Rubens is one of the great landmarks in the development of pure painting. This ebullient sensitive character brought fluidity to the art. His brush had a magic that gave it a swirling power. His pictures brim with movement. The brush strokes are long and liquid. Whatever criticisms are hurled at him, none can denigrate the power of his compositions, that can at their best abound with life and pure imaginative content. To examine a painting by Rubens is to glimpse many of the basic rules. Painting is first and foremost an art of brush strokes. The colours are given texture and form. Compare details by Rubens with close-ups of a portrait by the Dutchman, Frans Hals. Both men are on the same track. It can be noted again with the work of the Spaniard, Velasquez. Although from a few yards away the effect is of often meticulous likeness, as the picture is approached, the individual brush strokes that go to make-up this impression stand out. This is what painting is about, it is not something that is intended to follow the minute details of nature, but rather something of inspiration which is translated by the artist's mind and personal technique. Thus progress in painting to a large extent is based on an intimate knowledge of the materials, not only how colours react one against the other, but also the possibilities of intermixing. Most of all though, it is the brush and knife control which gives the key to success, and as more and more works by different masters are examined, it becomes evident how vital brushwork is. The strokes stand out as an individual handwriting, and in fact are one of the aids in identifying particular artists' work, although here the result can become blurred by the activities of the skilled forger.

As the sophistication of civilization advanced, tastes and education expanded: the fields for the artist widened and patronage became more enlightened. The Dutch School in itself contained masters who excelled in almost every branch of the subject. At the summit there was the giant figure of Rembrandt, who gave to his compositions, not only peerless drawing, but a unique and wonderful handling of light and shade. To study Rembrandt working away in his shadows, to note his control of highlight, and half-light and reflected-light, is to attend a master's lecture on these subjects. Note the gentle tonal changes that softly underline the detail in the shade. To Rembrandt not a minute area of the canvas is unimportant, every stroke and accent complements the final result. His subject coverage is immense – from stories from the Testaments to landscape; from catching the naive purity of a young boy's face to the delicate traceried statements of age.

Around Rembrandt there was a host of painters who left behind minor masterpieces: sea-painting, where the Van de Veldes work is well worth study; landscape by Hobbema and others, who were so much to influence the English East Anglian School later; interiors became exquisite jewels of quality in the hands of Vermeer, Metsu and de Hooch; the rollicking 'low life' is brought into rumbustious being by Steen; flowers by such as Van Huijsum. The list could run on for several pages.

The dictum of many teachers from the past was that to complete a successful art education, the student or victim should spend long days copying the works of masters. That idea has passed now; but a visual study of these same masters is most valuable for an understanding of techniques and materials. An exact copy of a passage does not have to be made, but it can be highly instructive and penetrating to note how a particular problem in a picture has been solved by the different masters. How foliage is rendered or suggested in a landscape mood by Nicholas Poussin in contrast with Gainsborough, Turner and Monet or Sisley. Each solved the problem in an individual manner, suited not only to his aesthetic approach but also to the manner in which the colour is handled. A quiet afternoon in a gallery can do much to increase not only knowledge, but also, perhaps, courage as well: for a close view can be taken of those who have pushed back the frontiers of expression and in so doing helped to lay a path for the later travellers. Do not for a moment try to ape what they have done; for to build a minor pastiche from the work of half-a-dozen major names will not assist personal progress; the result inevitably will be dull and the sources of the inspiration will stand out as trees in the desert. The secret is to make mental notes of the texture, colour changes, arrangement, and unusual composition manners. These mental-visual ideas can remain in the mind to fertilize your own ambitions, to support experiments – to flavour and to season as it were, but not to govern.

Composition is one of the most difficult aspects of painting to analyse; pointers can be given, but there are not many exact rulings that can be put forward which will guarantee success. The movement of shapes and principal bodies within the confines of the canvas or sheet of paper is largely a mentally controlled process. It is a thing of seeing balance and harmony, feeling out what is correct and what is out of sympathy. Again, turn to the galleries and see the

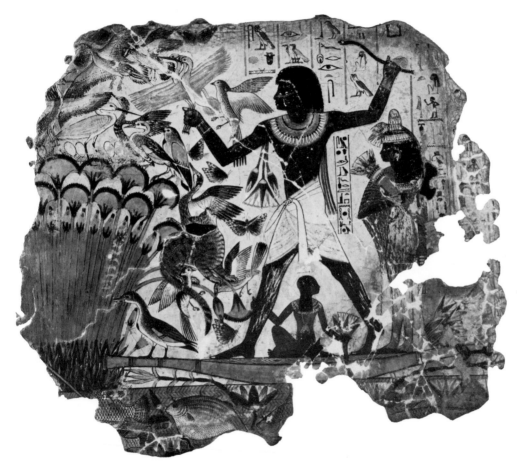

Theban tomb painting 18th dynasty.
Fowling in the marshes.
British Museum, London

problems tackled and how they have been answered. Notice the use of distortion, how it can lend strength and atmosphere; compare the work of El Greco with Cézanne and Modigliani. The artist should not be a slave to exact photographic image, rather is the construction and carrying through of a picture a challenge against which can be brought the full battery of individual talents.

The choice of medium has much to do with the final result. Between the most economic pure-wash methods and rich oil impasto lies a variety offering infinite experience for the painter. The meaning he desires to put over may be quietly lyrical, as the gentle watercolours of de Wint; it may be atmospheric as the superb expressions of Turner or the softer key studies of Whistler; it may be

13

flagrant flaming colour as with Matisse at his most flamboyant; or it may be the rugged texture of Van Gogh or the passionate emotion of Vlaminck. All these personal expressions were arrived at by long hours of experiment and exploration.

The exacting technique of tempera will not be dealt with here, as it calls for lengthy preparation of the surface or support, and also rigorously careful preparation of the colours, but it does have an affinity with gouache, which is described in a later chapter.

The arrival of the twentieth century has not only brought to light the huge number of would-be painters, but it has also produced the first new medium since the introduction of oil colours. This is the use of the pigments bound with an acrylic medium. One of the main advantages is that there is now available for the artist a medium which, with very few strictures, is virtually impossible to misuse. If only the discovery of acrylic vehicles for colours could have come a little earlier in the century, many fine works would not now be in danger of being lost. The twentieth century has been the great era of experimenting for artists, not only in composition and picture content, but also with additives to colours, particularly with oil paints that have been adulterated with plasters, unsuitable oils and the like, all of which have hastened their cracking, flaking and other impermanent characteristics.

When a painting is born, it is in the visual experience of the mind. Some aspect of a scene, a memory, a combination of colours, an atmospheric moment, triggers off a line of excitement that grows into the feel for a picture. To the artist his panel, canvas or sheet of paper becomes a window which will at the end of the day, or week, disclose a private view of a particular moment, arrangement, interior, scene or action. To visit an exhibition and pass through the rooms is to share a privileged moment with the great painters – to glance with them through this personal window, to stand and see from their stand-point.

Painting is one of the most natural of impulses, and the act can bring not only great satisfaction, but also a genuine fresh pleasure. The chapters that follow are for guidance in how to use materials, how to discover techniques: they are not in any way concerned with actually showing how to make pictures – that is the individual's contribution. An understanding of the use of brushes and colours, the characteristics of watercolour, gouache, oils and acrylics leave the way open. This knowledge is the servant for the creative impulses which are there trying to get out.

The materials

In painting, many of the materials are common to the different techniques. For a beginner a visit to the art shop is likely to cause confusion, as there is such a large array of colours, brushes, papers, oils and varnishes to choose from. In the following pages are brief descriptions of the majority of materials that will be met with, and some advice is offered to assist in making the choice.

Colours

The pigments used by painters fall into two categories. They may be either colours that are found in their natural state or those that are manufactured. Artists' colourmen today often list up to one hundred and fifty different colours, and a glance at a colour chart will show the advantages a twentieth-century painter has over his counterpart of five hundred years ago. The artist at the time of the Italian Renaissance had mostly to rely on pigments such as yellow ochre, the siennas, the umbers, vermilion, real ultramarine, terre verte, light red and unstable madders, greens, and various colours from plants. The first thing that would have amazed the painters of long ago would have been to see not only the variety of colours but their brightness and richness nowadays. Yet the painter still has to choose with care, for not all the colours offered are entirely permanent. It is regrettable that some pigments are highly unstable and it is still possible to buy asphaltum or bitumen, which brought about the downfall of so many pictures produced in the eighteenth and nineteenth centuries. Sir Joshua Reynolds, the first President of the Royal Academy, was a great experimenter with his materials and he fell a victim to the use of asphaltum. The pigment gives a delightful warm crimson brown and when used as a glaze behaved well until it started to dry out. A number of the paintings of the eighteenth and nineteenth centuries have a rugged craquelure somewhat similar to alligator-skin; this is often caused by asphaltum, which will not only bleed into the other colours but will also affect the varnish and disrupt the whole surface of a painting.

The following list gives the most important pigments. Some indication of their permanence when exposed to light and other influences, such as damp and chemical pollution in the air, is given by the number of asterisks placed after each name.

BLUES

Antwerp blue** A weaker form of Prussian blue, which is made by mixing Prussian blue with an inert filler or additive.

Cerulean blue**** This was introduced about 1870. It is a compound of cobalt and tin oxide. It is quite permanent in all media and has an attractive pale blue tint with a slight suggestion of green.

Cobalt blue**** This is a compound of aluminium oxide, cobalt oxide, and phosphoric acid. It is permanent in all media, and was discovered in France by Thénard in 1802. It is a bright, nearly transparent, colour but has a low tinting power. In oil painting it takes up to 100 per cent oil for grinding, but despite this it dries quickly; because of this fact it is liable to crack at times if overpainted on a layer that has not hardened out.

Cyanine blue** Prepared from Prussian blue and cobalt blue.

French ultramarine*** An artificial ultramarine made by heating clay, coal, soda and sulphur. It was first produced commercially by Guimet in France in 1828. It is normally reasonably permanent with all media for pictures or murals indoors, but its use for frescoes etc., out-of-doors, especially in towns or industrial areas, is not recommended as it can be affected by acid impurities in the air. It has the strange characteristic of tending to look darker by artificial light; this is, of course, an optical effect and not a physical one.

Indigo** This blue was originally made from a plant in the Middle East and India, but today is produced artificially as a derivative from coal tar. It is reasonably permanent with watercolour, but neither the natural nor the artificial indigo is suitable for oils.

Monastral blue*** This is prepared from copper phthalocyanine. Also called 'Monestial', 'Oxford' or 'Winsor' blue. One of the most recent discoveries, it is also one of the most powerful pigments. It has very strong tinting power, and for this reason the makers usually sell it with up to 90 per cent extender. It is a very useful addition to the palette and replaces in permanence and use Prussian blue, in all media. Mixed with colours such as alizarin crimson, burnt umber, cadmium yellow, it can produce very deep strong tones. It does have a slight tendency to dye hog bristles.

Prussian blue** Also known as Berlin blue and Paris blue, it is prepared from ferric ferrocyanide. This is a strong dark transparent blue with a slight green tinge. If it is used in a concentrated form, it tends to show a bronze tinge. It can be used with all media except fresco, as with this the lime will destroy it. With watercolour, if mixed with zinc white it will almost bleach out in strong light, but when placed in the dark will regain the former strength.

Smalt**** A ground-up potash glass which contains cobalt oxide. The final pigment has a very low tinting power, although it has a delicate attractive colour.

Today it is really replaced by cobalt blue.

Ultramarine****** This is produced by grinding the semi-precious stone lapis lazuli. Today it has been replaced by French ultramarine. The principal use is by restorers for retouching. The early masters used it with most media. Sometimes when it has been used with oils, it has a tendency to turn grey. The condition is called ultramarine sickness, but the truth is that the greyness is the appearance of clay and earth particles which were left with the pigment during the manufacturing process.

BROWNS

Bistre** It is made by charring beech wood; the resultant soot produces a pleasant warm brown colour. It was a great favourite with nineteenth-century watercolourists. Today it is better to use sepia.

Bone brown A warm crimson brown colour made by incompletely charring bones. It has a tarry nature which does not really dry and will cause the same type of troubles as asphaltum. It should not be used with any medium.

Brown madder*** This is prepared from one of the alizarins. It has a deep brown tone with a warm crimson tinge. It is more suitable for watercolour than oils in which medium it tends to dry very slowly.

Burnt sienna**** Raw sienna which has been calcined. It is completely safe with all media and has an attractive warm red-brown tint.

Burnt umber**** Raw umber that has been calcined. Absolutely permanent in all media except fresco out-of-doors when it does tend to decompose. It has a warm rich dark tint.

Raw sienna**** It is a native earth from Italy that contains hydrated ferric oxide. It is absolutely permanent in all media and has a tint approaching a very dark yellow ochre.

Raw umber**** A native earth that is found in Italy and Cyprus. Quite permanent in all media.

Sepia** The genuine colour is prepared from the ink produced by the cuttle-fish. This is not permanent. It tends to fade in bright light and is most suited to watercolour. The bulk of sepia sold today is a mixture of black and burnt sienna.

Vandyke brown** A native earth which can contain bitumen or rotted vegetable matter. It is unsuitable for oils and is not reliably permanent in watercolour.

GREENS

Alizarin green* This is a derivative of coal tar. It is liable to darken in bright light and is not recommended for any medium.

Cadmium green*** A powerful bright colour with strong tinting powers. It should replace doubtful colours such as Hooker's green and sap green.

Chrome green** It is prepared from a mixture of chrome yellow and Prussian blue or monastral blue. It has at times a rather unpleasant acid tint. It could be replaced by cadmium green.

Cobalt green**** This is prepared from cobalt zincate and zinc oxide. It has a pleasant bluish grey tint. It is opaque but has little strength of tone. Quite safe in all media.

Emerald green** Produced from copper aceto-arsenite. It has a clear slightly bluish green tint. It is liable to be impermanent with pigments such as cadmium yellow and vermilion which contain sulphur. It is wisest to 'break' it with titanium white only. It is also one of the most poisonous pigments obtainable.

Hooker's green** It is made from a mixture of Prussian blue and gamboge. It is not permanent in any medium. There is however a present-day substitute made from coal tar which is fairly safe in watercolour.

Monastral green*** This is prepared from chlorinated copper phthalocyanine. It is also called Monestial or Winsor green. A powerful colour similar in tint to viridian. The same remarks apply as for monastral blue.

Olive green** The original was an impermanent mixture of raw sienna and ultramarine or Prussian blue. It is now made from a mixture of raw sienna with monastral green. It is not safe in oils but is reasonably permanent in watercolour.

Oxide of chromium**** Anhydrous chromic oxide. A cool opaque green and one of the safest colours in all media. It has a strong tinting power and covers well.

Sap green** The original colour was completely fugitive, being made from unripe buckthorn berries. Today sap green is made from a derivative of coal tar. It is not a very good colour and could be simulated from monastral green and cadmium yellow.

Terre verte**** A native green earth which contains both ferric and ferrous oxides. It is quite permanent in all media, although it has very little tinting power.

Viridian**** This is prepared from chromium hydroxide. It has a pleasant deep cool green tint and is quite permanent in all media. It came into use about 1862.

GREYS

Charcoal grey*** This is made from various charcoals and can vary from cool to warm brown greys. It does not grind up very smoothly and is not suitable as a pigment for any medium, but has some value for light washes in watercolour.

Davy's gray**** This is prepared from powdered slate and can vary greatly in colour. It is permanent and works quite well in watercolour but brushes out badly with oil.

Neutral tint*** It is made from a mixture of alizarin crimson, French ultramarine and a black. Only suitable with watercolours.

Payne's gray*** As with neutral tint, a mixed colour. In watercolour it has a similar recipe to that of neutral tint, but with oils it is made up from French ultramarine, yellow ochre and ivory black.

PURPLES

Alizarin violet* It is prepared from a derivative of coal tar. A permanent bright transparent colour in all media.

Cobalt violet** Originally, in the nineteenth century, this was extracted from a rare ore. Today it is made from cobalt arsenate or cobalt phosphate. If it is the first of these, it is very poisonous. The second is non-poisonous and quite safe in any medium.

Magenta* An aniline lake, which is impermanent in all media.

Mars violet** An artificial oxide of iron. Quite permanent and most suitable for use in oils.

Mauve* Similar to magenta.

Mineral violet** A very strong pigment. Most suited to oils.

Purple lake* A strong colour with a slight blue tinge prepared from the alizarins. Not really reliable in any medium.

Purple madder* Prepared from alizarin and not wholly reliable in any medium.

Violet alizarin* As for purple madder.

REDS

Cadmium red* This is prepared from cadmium sulphide and cadmium selenide. It can be bought in two or more depths of tone. It is completely permanent and the lighter tone replaces vermilion, which can have impermanent qualities.

Carmine* The original lake colour was produced from the cochineal insect found in Central America. It can be affected by strong light, particularly with oils. In watercolour, if applied in a very thin wash, it seems to last better. The natural colour has now been replaced by one of the alizarins.

Crimson alizarin* Lake alizarin, red alizarin, scarlet alizarin. These transparent colours are all produced from anthracene, a derivative of coal tar. They replace many of the old plant-based lakes. They dry very slowly in oils.

Crimson lake* Originally a derivative of carmine, and as such was fugitive. It is now made from one of the alizarins and is distinguished from alizarin crimson by a very slightly blue tinge.

Harrison red* A bright cherry red which is affected by light. Cadmium red should be substituted.

Indian red** It is prepared from iron oxides. It has a subtle blue tinge and is quite permanent.

Light red** Prepared from calcined yellow ochre and the tint will vary with the ochre used.

Madder lake* Prepared from the root of the madder plant. Only suitable for pale watercolour washes.

Mars red** A synthetic oxide of iron, best suited to oils.

Rose dore* At one time a derivative from rose madder. It is now replaced by one of the alizarins.

Rose madder* Originally made as a derivative from madder. It will fade with strong light and has now been replaced by one of the alizarins.

Scarlet lake* At one time this was a mixture of vermilion and cochineal. Not very long ago it was made from an aniline base. It should now be replaced by alizarin scarlet.

Venetian red** Originally this was found as an earth-containing iron oxide. Today it is prepared from ferric oxide with a little calcium sulphate. It has a slight bluish tinge very like Indian red. It is liable to dry with a brittle film in oils.

Vermilion* It is made from mercuric sulphide and is extremely poisonous. True vermilion has a delicate blue-grey tinge that has always been very popular with portrait painters for mixing the gentle skin tones of the female face. It can behave erratically and darken with light and time. It has largely been replaced by cadmium red.

YELLOWS

Aureolin* It is prepared from cobalt-potassium nitrite. It is a transparent yellow, most suitable for watercolour, although can be used for glazing with oils. It replaces gamboge.

Cadmium yellow* This is produced from cadmium sulphide in several different tints. They all have very strong tinting powers and replace the chrome yellows. Cadmium orange is made by an addition of cadmium selenide. Both colours are safe in all media.

Chrome yellow* It is prepared from lead chromate and was introduced towards the end of the eighteenth century. Chrome yellows and oranges tend to darken, especially with oils.

Gamboge* Watercolour only. A native yellow gum derived from a species of Garcinia growing in Siam. It is transparent and although it has been used from medieval times is liable to fade.

Indian yellow* This was made originally in India by evaporating urine of cows that had eaten mango leaves. The present-day colour is a derivative of coal tar with rather suspect permanence.

Mars yellow* An artifial oxide of iron. Quite permanent in any medium.

Naples yellow* This is made from lead antimonate and is highly poisonous. It is most suitable for oils.

Permanent yellow* **Lemon yellow*** These are both prepared from barium chromate.

Roman ochre** A dark variety of ochre.

Yellow ochre**** A native earth coloured by iron oxide. Depending on where the earth comes from, it can have a wide range of dull yellow tints. It is completely permanent in any medium.

BLACKS

Blue-black**** It is made by calcining wood and other plant materials. It has a cool blue tinge.

Bone black** It is produced by charring bones. It has a warm brown tint but lacks permanence by comparison with the other blacks.

Ivory black**** Originally the best quality was made by charring ivory chips. Today it is largely made from bones. It is one of the best blacks with any medium, but care is needed with oils, as if it is laid over a white ground it may crack. This condition can be avoided by mixing a very small part of another dark colour, such as burnt umber, with the ivory black.

Lamp black**** This is almost pure carbon and is made by collecting soot from burning oil. Permanent in any medium.

Peach black**** A vegetable black with a subtle brown tinge.

Vine black**** Prepared from charred vine roots. It is suitable for all media except fresco.

WHITES

Chinese white**** A zinc white suitable for watercolour or gouache only. It was introduced into England about 1830.

Flake white*** also known as Cremnitz white and silver white. It is based on lead carbonate and is a cumulative poison. It is very opaque and suitable only for oils or tempera. If used with watercolour, it is liable to darken where the air is heavily polluted.

Foundation white*** A heavy opaque white, mainly used for priming and underpainting.

Titanium white*** Is made from titanium oxide. It is a very good coverer, non-poisonous and works well with all media. The most recently introduced white pigment.

Zinc white*** This is prepared from zinc oxide. It is less opaque than flake or titanium white, but it does not dry very well with oils and can form a hard brittle skin.

The foregoing list of colours has been given so that the main range available can be appreciated and understood. For making a start with acrylics, water-colour or oils, the following colours will be quite sufficient:

Cadmium yellow, yellow ochre, cadmium red, Indian red, alizarin crimson,

French ultramarine, viridian, raw umber, burnt umber, and titanium white.

These nine colours and the white, with intermixes, will provide ample tints

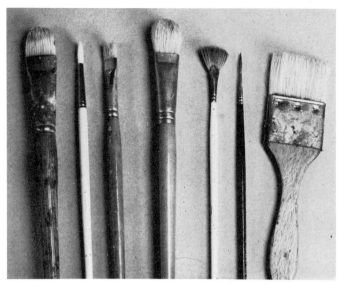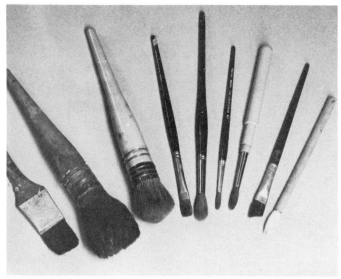

Above left. Oil, Acrylic and Alkyd painting brushes. (Left to right) A so-called Rubens shape, with bristles curved inwards to give strong control for long strokes. Small Round hog-bristle. Small Flat hog-bristle. Large Filbert; this shape is a a cross between a Round and a Flat. A Sweetener, fan-shaped and made from sable hair, used for blending colours or flattening down impasto. A Rigger made from long sable hairs for detail work. A flat hog-bristle Varnishing brush.

Above right. Watercolour brushes. (Left to right) Chinese brush that can be goat, badger or sometimes dog. Here it is set in a bamboo handle. A Sword or Cut made of ox-hair. A Round sable set in a plastic handle, the thick part of which comes off and screws on over the brush head for travelling. Small Round sable. Large Round sable. Flat sable. Round Mop in ox-hair. Extra large Mop in pony hair. Flat Mop in squirrel.

and tones for any subject that will be met with. It is simpler to obtain colour harmony working with a comparatively restricted list than with the palette ringed with two or three dozen colours. To paint successfully, an intimate knowledge of the colours used is necessary. At the start, take time to practise mixing the colours and find out how they react and exactly what tints can be made.

Brushes

The expertly made brushes that can be bought so easily today would have been the envy of painters two or three hundred years ago who had to make their own or train their apprentices to do this. The first examples known of a manufactured paint brush come from Egypt and date from about 2000 B.C. These were made using rush fibres and were bound with cord to a wooden handle. Since that time artists have experimented with a wide variety of materials: animal bristles and hairs, baleen from whales, vegetable fibres and synthetic bristles.

The painter's brush today falls into one of two categories: first, hog bristle, which for the better brush is white, for the cheaper is from black bristle; secondly, hair, for which, in the case of the most expensive, guard hairs from the kolinsky (sable) are used, and cheaper qualities are made from ox hair, squirrel, pony and ringcat.

When buying brushes of any sort, always examine them carefully to make certain the bristles and hairs are set properly. Good brushes should last many years. They should be thoroughly cleaned after painting sessions, and the heads should be gently re-set with the finger tips. If they are put away for any length of time, a small amount of moth repellent should be put close to them, as the clothes' moth will make an attack.

The principal shapes for brushes are: 1) *round* 2) *flat* 3) *filbert*, this last is a cross in shape between the round and the flat. Other specialist shapes include the *sword* which with its bevelled edge is useful for long-line work, the *rigger* for detail with oils, the *sweetener* for blending with oils, acrylic or gouache, the *mop* which is often made of badger hair and is mainly intended for large areas of wash work, and the *oriental*, this last has goat or badger hair set, generally, in a bamboo handle with the hairs coming to a very fine point, and it is intended to be held at right angles to the paper to produce the typical brush-marks of the oriental artists. They will be found only in specialist shops.

A brush is not just an instrument for putting on paint, it is the means of making the paint marks say something. A brush-stroke is just as much drawing as a careful outline with a sharp pencil. Each of the main brush shapes has very definite characteristics. Practise using each brush in a variety of ways. Hold it first underhand. Hold it sideways. Find out what happens to the paint when the brush is twisted, and when it is stippled straight down. Note the difference between the strokes of the flat brush when it is held at two different angles.

For making a start with acrylics or oils, these five brushes will be sufficient – they should all be of good quality white hog bristle: two *round*, a size *number 2*

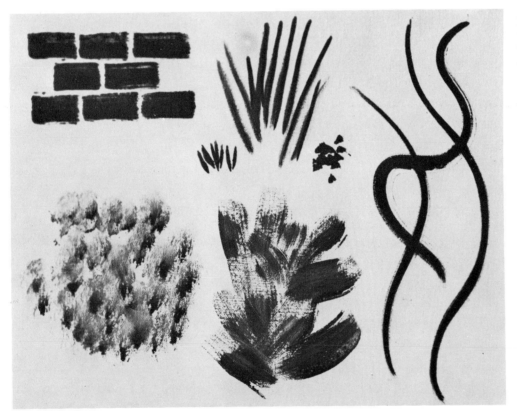

Assorted strokes with hog-brushes. The more experimenting that can be done the richer and more satisfying will be the finished picture. Try making each stroke draw completely as with the blocks at the top left.

for drawing and details, a *number 8* for broader work; a *number 6 filbert* shape, and *numbers 4* and *6 flat* shape. For working with watercolour or diluted application of acrylics use: a *number 3* and a *number 8 round* sable brushes, $\frac{3}{4}''$ (18 mm) *flat* ox-hair, and also include a large *mop*, which can be from squirrel or ringcat.

A selection of painting and palette knives. The blades should always be of pliant steel and when the handles are cranked this should be sufficient to allow the knuckles of the holding hand to clear the surface of the canvas or panel.

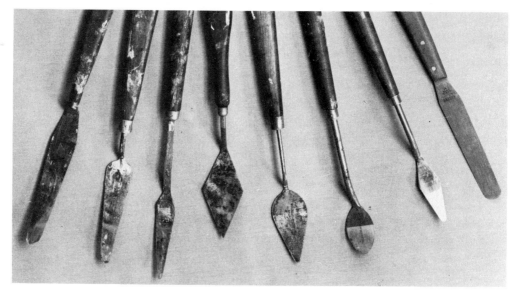

Knives

Painting knives for the application of acrylics or oils will widen the scope of the technique. There are two points to watch for when buying a painting knife: the first is to see that the blade is made of pliable elastic steel, so that it will be possible to make a sensitive stroke; the second, that the handle is sufficiently cranked, so that the fingers of the hand holding the knife will be clear of the paint surface. These painting knives come in many designs ranging from quite small trowels with a blade about $\frac{3}{4}''$ (18 mm) long up to those with $4''$ or $5''$ (102 or 131 mm) blades. To start with, two of contrasting shape will be sufficient and more can be bought as progress is made. For cleaning up the palette after acrylic or oils, a straightforward palette knife is a help. But an old kitchen knife will manage very well if the blade is first blunted.

Impasto marks from differing painting knives. The technique here should be as direct as possible because going back over the work will destroy the freshness.

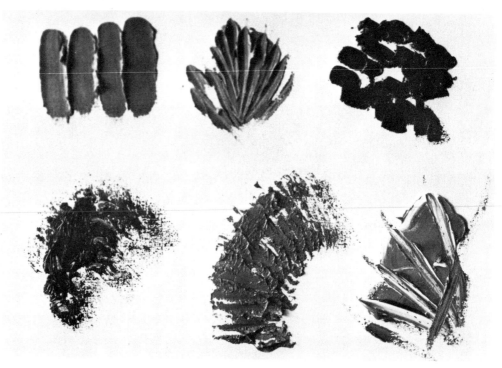

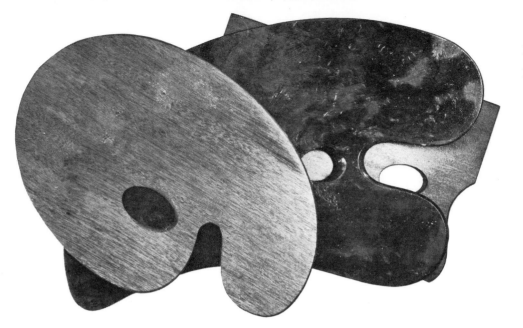

Palettes

The traditional artist's mahogany palette comes in three different shapes: the rectangular, the hooked, the balanced studio. The rectangular is often supplied with paintboxes or paintbox-easels as it serves for a lid to keep the colours in place. It is not so comfortable to hold as the other two but is more convenient for carrying around. The choice between a hooked and balanced palette is a personal one. The balanced generally is the larger of the two and certainly sits comfortably on your arm when working for long periods.

Most art dealers will carry a fair selection of ceramic palettes for water-colours. These will include almost flat tiles with shallow depressions, small individual saucers or larger versions of the same shape with two, three or more

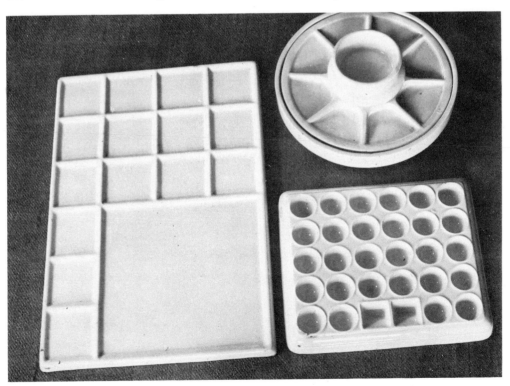

Porcelain palettes. The example to the left is a flat tile measuring ten by fourteen inches (25 × 35 cm). Bottom right has deep wells and is suitable for acrylic colours as it lends itself to covering. Top right has central water container.

divisions and elaborate examples with interchangeable colour holders and a water cup. There can also be seen numerous plastic palettes, which are generally much cheaper and, although they may stain with some of the colours, will serve very well. One of the most useful is a so-called 'patty-pan', which resembles a cake baking tin with six, eight or twelve cups. When working with washes, one of these is most useful.

Other palettes that can be suitable for all three media are made of sheets of formica, enamelled tin, and packs of disposable greaseproof paper sheets.

For oil painting, many find a dipper is an advantage. This is a small metal cup for holding oil or medium that can be clipped on to the edge of the palette.

Supports

Paper By repute it was the Chinese who first made paper somewhere about the end of the first century. The first papers to come to Europe arrived about the eleventh century and this opened the way not only for the encouragement of drawing and watercolour but also made possible the start of print-making. The two principal types of paper are cartridge, which is made from wood pulp, and rag paper. With the latter, linen or cotton rags are cut up into small pieces and these fragments are then boiled together whilst being agitated to break them down and separate the fibres. The resulting pulp, or 'stuff', as it is known in the trade, is then ready for the paper maker, who lowers a sieve into the 'stuff' and manipulates it so that a layer of a definite thickness is lifted out. This is then left to dry and the sheet of paper has been made. Although purists demand that no additives should really be put into the 'stuff', today size is often added to assist the adhesion of the fibres, and caustic soda to hasten the breakdown of the rags.

When buying sheets of rag paper it will be noticed that the thickness of the paper is indicated by the description – 90 lbs., 65 lbs., etc. per ream of 480 sheets (in metric – grammes per square metre = gsm).

The surface of rag paper can be 'hot pressed', 'not' and 'rough'. 'Hot pressed' will have been ironed to give it a glossy surface; 'not' or 'cold pressed' will have been left mat; and 'rough' will either have been artificially roughened or the texture will have been produced in the sieving.

Paper for the artist used to be made to a name for a given size, the principal being:

Half Imperial	15 × 22 inches	Elephant	23 × 28 inches
Royal	19 × 24 inches	Double Elephant	26½ × 40 inches
Super Royal	19¼ × 27 inches	Antiquarian	31 × 53 inches
Imperial	22 × 30 inches		

But in the art shops you will now find International sizes which are:

A0 841 × 1189 mm/$33\frac{1}{8}$ × $46\frac{3}{4}$ inches
A1 841 × 594 mm/$33\frac{1}{8}$ × $23\frac{3}{8}$ inches
A2 420 × 594 mm/$16\frac{1}{2}$ × $23\frac{3}{8}$ inches
A3 420 × 297 mm/$16\frac{1}{2}$ × $11\frac{3}{4}$ inches
A4 210 × 297 mm/ $8\frac{1}{4}$ × $11\frac{3}{4}$ inches
A5 210 × 148 mm/ $8\frac{1}{4}$ × $5\frac{1}{8}$ inches

If larger sheets are needed, they will have to be in cartridge, which can be bought in rolls up to five feet (762 mm) wide and twenty-five or fifty yards (22.9 or 45.7 m) long.

Besides white papers, there are a number of tinted and textured papers that can be found. These include oriental papers from China and India made from bamboo shoots, or mulberry leaves. Many of these papers have delightful broken surfaces, which can be incorporated in the technique. There are also what are known as pasteless boards for watercolour and gouache; these have the advantage that they have considerable thickness and will not need to be stretched.

Canvases, Panels and Easels These are discussed in the chapters on acrylics and oils.

Acrylic paints

Since the introduction of oil painting, for about five hundred years no new medium for the artist had been found. The explosive techniques and widening creative expression of the twentieth century put demands upon the established media of oil and watercolour that they were not entirely able to meet. Many painters today want to be able to work with complete freedom without having to worry about the mechanics of technique or to be troubled with lengthy preparation of the painting surface – canvas, board or paper – also known as supports. In 1960 Acrylic paints were introduced for artists and largely met the demands above. In 1976 Alkyd colours have been developed to give further scope, particularly for artists wishing to employ oil techniques.

Acrylic paints

When these colours were introduced they opened up immediately many new fields for exploration. First and foremost it is essential that acrylic painting is approached as a completely new medium. The paints by their constitution have different characteristics from oil or watercolours. If an attempt is made to use them either as oils or watercolour, the result is likely to bring disappointment. What the manufacturers have done is to develop a medium for the artist that to a certain extent relieves him of much of the basic preparation technique worries. The boards or paper to be used with acrylics do not necessarily need special grounds and priming. The acrylic colours, even when applied very thickly, will not crack.

Basically acrylic colours are so called when they use a polymer emulsion as a vehicle; that is, instead of grinding the pigments with linseed oil, as with oil colours, or a water-soluble gum, as for watercolours, the pigments are milled with an emulsion of polyvinyl acetate and acrylic resin. The resins used with these new colours that appear under a wide variety of trade names are synthetic and were first developed by the American firm of Rohm and Haas in the early twenties. But it was not until after the war, despite the fact that these synthetic resins had been used for many industrial processes, that the artists' colourmen began to experiment with the possibility of their use as a vehicle for pigments.

The fact that the acrylic medium is an emulsion to a certain extent gives the working qualities of acrylics a relationship with those of egg tempera. As the acrylic colours are emulsion-bound they can be diluted with water, but as with egg tempera they cannot and should never be mixed with other media or their permanence and working qualities will be affected. On no account should acrylics ever be mixed with oil or spirits similar to turpentine, or gumlike substances. The only liquid additives should be either water or one or other of the acrylic mediums recommended by the manufacturers. If these rules are adhered to, the resulting properties of the acrylic paints will include high-speed drying, imperviousness to water, strength, and a permanently flexible film.

The surfaces that acrylics may be used on include almost every material that painters have ever used. It should be remembered that the basic acrylic medium which is mixed with the pigments is itself a very powerful adhesive. All types of paper, from thin newsprint and shelf-paper to good quality cartridge and rag papers and tinted pastel and sugar papers, can be used. The thinner types of paper can first be treated with acrylic medium by itself or with acrylic primer. This will not only greatly increase the tensile strength but in the case of the primer will provide an even ground over a broken or printed surface. Both the medium and the primer will be found to dry out quickly and under normal conditions the paper will be ready to paint on within an hour. The principal factor that affects the drying speed of acrylics is the relative humidity or moisture content of the air; therefore, on a damp, cold day the drying time may be increased up to two or three hours, but, once the medium, primer or colour has dried the resulting film should be waterproof.

The various man-made boards, hardboard, strawboard, pasteboard, and different cards, are all suitable. It is not necessary to prime these first, as the

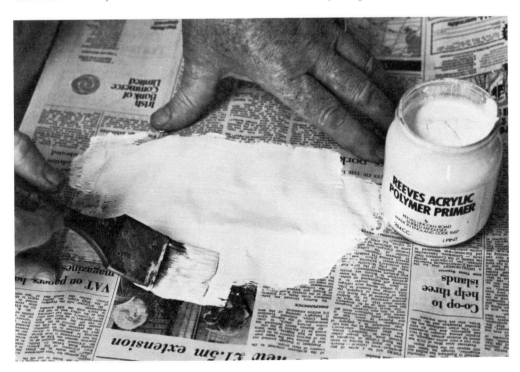

Acrylic primer being applied to newspaper. It has excellent covering power, as can be seen; also the acrylic will considerably strengthen a weak paper such as this.

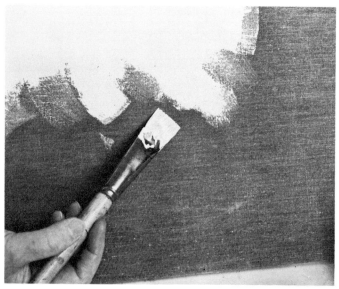 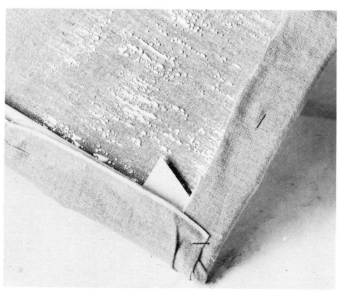

Left. Raw canvas, hessian, sacking, sailcloth and similar materials can be satisfactorily primed with acrylic primer for use with acrylics, alkyds or oils. The primer can be put on straight out of the pot or if a smoother surface is desired several applications of the primer can be made when it has been diluted with water. If rougher textures are wanted substances such as whiting, sand and inert plasters can be mixed with the primer.

Right. When priming coarse textiles, the layer can be given added security by putting heavy pressure on the brush and forcing the primer through so that it locks round the fibres.

colours will safely adhere to the untouched surfaces. However, the application of a coat of acrylic primer does give a more pleasant surface upon which to paint and on a heavily absorbent material it will certainly mean that the colours will have greater flow and ease of brushing. One point is important; if a thin board is being used to paint on and it is of a size more than about 16″ (400 mm) × 12″ (300 mm), it should really be strengthened with wood battens to prevent warping at a later stage. When using hardboard it is a matter of personal taste as to whether the smooth or the rough side is painted on; but it is worth re-membering that the rough side with its mechanical texture will not only take up a lot of paint but will also tend to leave the monotonous pattern of the machine-made texture showing through all but the thickest paint.

Wooden panels can be prepared with acrylics. The main factor here is to make sure that the wood chosen is fully seasoned and all accretions of resins and sap are absent. A safety measure can be to wipe over the surface of the wood with a piece of cotton wool soaked in methylated spirits, which will remove free resin and quickly evaporate. Here again, it is not necessary to prime the wood; it is a matter for the personal choice of technique. The applica-tion of thin glazed techniques over woods with pronounced grains offers fields for experiment which just would not be possible with the other media. If a priming is desired, it may be made using a wide soft-haired brush to produce a gesso-like smoothness, or it may be given a medium texture by applying it with a felt-covered roller. A heavier texture still can be produced by pressing a piece of coarse sacking into the wet priming and then pulling it away. As with hard-board panels, those made from wood should be battened if there is a danger of buckling. It is inadvisable to use three-ply panels as with the passing of time these are almost certain to attract the attention of woodworm.

Textiles for centuries have been one of the materials most favoured for painting on. The materials to be chosen from include hessian, sacking, linen, cotton, sailcloth, muslin, and any type of canvas woven from a natural fibre. Broadly speaking fabrics from man-made fibres are not satisfactory, as surface dressings can interfere with the adhesion of the colours and also there can be unpredictable movements of these cloths. Some of them can be affected by acid and other pollutants in the atmosphere. It is important with any textile that it should be adequately supported before painting on it. It is unwise to paint upon a piece of canvas and then stretch it or mount it afterwards, because it is practically impossible to do this without causing stresses and strains on the paint-film, which could cause the film to lift. The canvas or other material should either be mounted on a wooden stretcher or stuck on to a piece of hardboard or a wooden panel. This latter mounting can be done using acrylic medium or by laying it into a bed of acrylic primer. Depending upon the painting technique again, the textile support may be used either unprimed or primed.

If very thin materials like muslin, organdie or silk have been selected and no noticeable primer is desired, but it is felt a slight stiffening or strengthening is needed, this can be given by gently brushing on or spraying on a mixture of half water and half acrylic medium. When very coarse or open-weave sacking is used, a heavy coat of priming should first be applied. This should be done by pushing the brush well into the material to force the priming through so that it locks round the individual fibres. It is underlined here that on no account should any oil-based primers ever be used for acrylics. This includes household undercoat paints and, generally speaking, many of the advertised emulsion paints. This latter is mentioned as a safeguard, as the constituents may be at variance with those of the acrylic colours. Most artists' colourmen have ready-constituted acrylic primers and these are the only satisfactory and safe materials to use. These primers, however, can be diluted with water or acrylic medium if a thinner consistency is needed; they can also be stiffened or have their texture altered by the addition of substances such as kaolin, marble dust or whiting. It is normally safe to do this working on a ratio of one part additive to four parts primer.

Metal and glass may also be used with acrylics for painting on; the most important thing here is, to make sure that their surfaces have been completely degreased; this can be done by wiping over with pieces of cotton wool soaked in methylated spirits. Metal sheets, which may be of aluminium, copper or zinc, can be first slightly roughened by rubbing with sand or emery papers. Steel sheet is not suitable as it will rust and throw off the paint. The acrylic paint film, although waterproof in itself, by its molecular structure is not air-tight and therefore does not prevent oxidization of the steel underneath.

Another metal which has considerable possibilities for use as an under-support for acrylics is gold. In the past, particularly four or five hundred years ago, the painters of icons and early religious formal groups showed how many colours took on beautiful rich effects when placed against the gold. The gold-leaf must be correctly laid on a gesso ground which is absolutely smooth and flat. This gesso may be of the traditional plaster and animal glue mix, or it may be prepared using a binder of one part acrylic medium to two parts of water mixed with kaolin, marble dust or whiting. The gold-leaf can be laid on to the gesso using a wide soft-hair flat brush known as a 'tip' and stuck into position with glair or acrylic medium broken down with one part of medium to three parts of water. After the whole has hardened out, if a full gold sheen surface is called for, the gold-leaf can be burnished with a piece of agate.

Glazed surfaces, including china, earthenware, and formica, can be painted on with acrylics. They should not, however, be considered to have the same permanence as the supports that have already been mentioned. As with glass and metal the surfaces should be carefully degreased with methylated spirits.

Mural painting, except for true fresco, has always posed problems of permanence. Oil paint, with its impermeable film, is not suitable and various combinations of casein, gum and forms of tempera cannot always be reliable. Acrylic colours have many features to commend them for internal mural paintings. The wall surfaces that can be considered suitable include cement, concrete, gesso, marble, plaster, slate and stone. Wall surfaces can vary considerably. Over-dry conditions can make the surface layers powdery and loose. Over-damp can cause impenetrable paint layers to be thrown off. The acrylic colours are best applied thinned with acrylic medium or water or a mixture of both to suit the particular technique. Before starting to paint, a coat of acrylic primer should be put on over the whole wall; if possible this should be allowed to harden out for twenty-four hours. If the surface of the wall is loose, it should be given one or two coats of a mixture of half and half acrylic medium and water, allowing twenty-four hours between each application; the effect of this is that the acrylic medium will sink in and consolidate the top layers of the plaster. If the surface is very loose, the first coat can be applied by a spray. Cracks or chips that are missing can be filled in with a paste made from whiting or marble dust with acrylic medium. After the consolidation the priming is then applied.

It is possible and reasonably safe practice to paint with acrylic colours either as they are out of the tube or diluted with medium or water straight on to sandstone, slate, limestone or other rock or stone surfaces to be found in interior work. It should be noted that if the material is hygroscopic, like sandstone or limestone, the colour is very liable to sink quite deeply into the stone and would be almost impossible to remove. If a mistake is made, the excess should be quickly sponged away with water and then if it is important that the error is completely removed, a paste of sepiolite and water should be made and applied over the spot. As it dries the evaporation will tend to pull the stain out of the stone into the sepiolite. If this fails, a second remedy could be to use a paste of sepiolite mixed with clear industrial methylated spirits.

The use of acrylic colours for external work is not strongly recommended, as factors such as an excess of heat from the sun's rays, air pollution and excessive rain could affect the paint film. Excessive heat does tend to weaken the adhesion, and long continuous rain, although it would not affect the actual colours, could seep through the film, which breathes, and cause it to become detached from the wall.

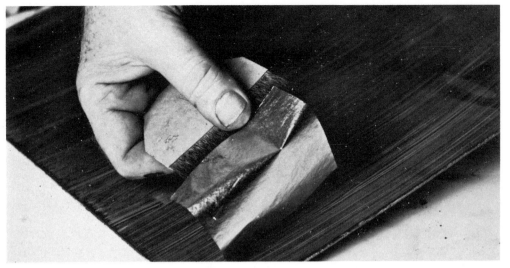

There are no such things as special brushes just for the use of acrylics. The personal technique of a painter and experimentation will decide which are the best types. The important point to watch with brushes is that they are completely cleaned after use. If this is done right away, it is simply a matter of rinsing in plenty of clean cold water. Normally it will not be necessary to use warm water and soap. If, however, the acrylic colour is allowed to dry hard into the bristles or hair, water will not remove the hard colour. Clogged brushes should be left to soak for an hour or more in methylated spirits; after this they should be well rinsed free of spirit and then washed out with a little plain soap and lukewarm water. Painting and palette knives may also be used for applying the paint, and hardened colour can be easily scraped from these with a sharp knife or stiff razor blade.

The choice of palette may be from glass, porcelain, formica, or fired enamel surfaces. Wood is not suitable, for the acrylic medium, being a strong adhesive, is very difficult to clean from wood, and if the colour dried out it would be almost impossible to remove without damaging the palette. Probably a sheet of plate glass is the most satisfactory for studio use. A piece cut to the size of the painting table will allow for plenty of room for mixing and also can be very easily cleaned. If the colours harden they can be simply removed by sluicing the palette with hot water, which will normally make them peel away. The disposable paper palette is quite suitable for outside work and is very convenient.

In painting with acrylics, it has already been mentioned that liquid other than water or acrylic medium should NOT be mixed with the colours. The reason for this is, that the binding vehicle is very carefully formulated as an emulsion and the permanence and working qualities of this vehicle can be upset by contact or mixing with oils, spirits or grease. The various makers produce different varieties of acrylic medium to add to the colours. These include: glossy medium, mat and glazing mediums. The first, if mixed with the colours, will tend to increase the sheen and it may also be used as a final varnish after the painting has dried out. The glazing medium is intended to increase the flow and transparency when using the glazing colours.

When working with acrylic colours, drying out on the palette can be slowed down by placing several thicknesses of well-damped clean rag over the wells holding the colours.

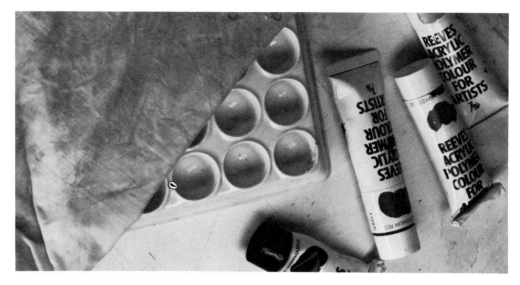

Acrylic paints can be bought in metal or plastic tubes, glass jars or plastic squeeze bottles. As the colours are liable to dry out quickly when exposed to the air, it is important to watch that tube caps and jar tops are kept firmly in place whenever not being used. For long life in the paint-box, metal tubes are probably the best as they can be squeezed up from the bottom and it is possible to make sure all the air is excluded.

In the previous chapter, a short list of colours was suggested and if these are kept to during the preliminary stages, much valuable experience can be built up. Further, working from a few colours is far less wasteful than having a dozen or more ringing the palette.

Objections have been raised against acrylic colours that they do dry out too quickly. Earlier in this chapter it was said that acrylics are quite a new medium. This speed of drying is one of the characteristics of that medium and it can obviously be exploited in a number of ways. However, if a slower drying colour is wanted, a retarder can be bought which will slow down the drying speed very considerably. Colours on the palette can be kept in a workable condition for appreciably longer periods by gently spraying with water, or in between painting sessions a damp cloth can be laid over them to prevent evaporation. If working on a large scale, a deep-well palette can be used, which can be effectively sealed off with a sheet of polythene or similar cover.

The principal attraction of acrylics for the painter is their ability to be used in a very wide variety of manners. As has been mentioned, almost any type of surface is safe and suitable. The medium, however, if it is to be exploited thoroughly, does need to be experimented with and understood. Just as with watercolour and gouache, oil-painting, glaze and impasto effects can be simulated, so, quite obviously, similar manners can be imitated. There will be, of course, subtle differences in the individual behaviour of the various pigments and these can be appreciated only by mixing and painting with the colours.

How do the colours react together? As the pigments that are mixed with the acrylic medium are the same as those for watercolour or oil, the actual mixing and results will be the same.

Acrylics present a challenge to the artist. Here at last is a medium that does not rely on pre-set disciplines of application that for many tend to limit the means of expression. In the following pages will be outlined the principal ways of painting and at the end some of the allied uses for acrylics.

Wash

Before starting to paint with heavily diluted colours, if working on a paper it should be stretched. Initial drawing is best carried out with a small round sable or soft-hair brush using a weak neutral mixture of umber and ultramarine. The strokes should be very pale, so much so that at the end of the picture they will hardly show, if at all. This initial drawing should be kept to the absolute minimum; it should be no more than the barest bones of the composition. The more pre-drawing that is done before painting, the more the final result will tend to look tight and constricted.

Prior to putting on the washes, make sure that plenty of colour is mixed and is ready in a deep-well palette or series of plastic cups and jars. Once a wash has been started it is a hazardous business to stop whilst fresh supplies of colour are mixed up. If the wash is being applied to heavy card or paper that has not been stretched, the whole surface of the paper or card should be sponged over with clean water to remove excess size and dust. The surface may then be allowed to dry or not, as wished. A moist surface will take a wash more easily and quickly than a dry, and a perfectly flat finish can often be achieved more easily in this way.

The board should be given about a five degree tilt. Then, using the largest available soft-hair brush, the wash should be begun from the top of the paper or card. The secret is to put on sufficient weight of colour and water so that with just a little guidance from the brush, the colour itself will gradually flow down the surface. Gradations from dark to light can be achieved by adding brushfuls of clean water; and from light to dark by adding a stronger tone of the same colour which is ready-mixed in another compartment on the palette. Once the wash is complete the board can be laid flat on the table, and exciting 'bleed' effects achieved by dripping other colours into the moist wash; these can be further manipulated by strokes from the brush.

It is possible to bring out light areas in a wet wash by the use of clean white blotting paper, pieces of cotton wool or clean soft cotton rag. If a mistake has been made the area should be well sluiced with clean water and then blotted and the process repeated several times. If the mistake is still not removed a further attempt can be made by gently rubbing clear industrial methylated spirits into the area and again blotting. After this the part of the picture affected should be washed with clean water before carrying on painting.

To get the purest effect with wash work, as far as possible transparent colours or near transparent colours should be used. With this procedure charming and subtle tints can be achieved by, for example, washing a yellow over a blue to produce a green, or a yellow over a red to produce an orange.

The difference that will be noticed when working with acrylics as opposed to watercolour in wash work is that the acrylics are more fluid and they do not bleed so freely into one another.

Opaque

For the application of slightly thicker colours, paints as they come from the tube or pot should be thinned with one or other of the acrylic mediums depending on what the final effect is to be. The fact that the acrylic mediums are milky and opaque when in their liquid state should not cause concern as this milkiness disappears when they dry out. This can be simply proved by brushing a thin layer of one of the mediums on to a sheet of glass, and it will be found that when dry it will be completely clear and can be lifted off with a razor blade as a thin sheet of clear plastic.

The application of strong or weak-toned opaque colours should be done as directly as possible, letting the individual stroke give the impression of what is being imitated; for example, a flat brush held in one way can simulate brick-work, held in another with short sharp thin strokes it can make marks that resemble reeds.

Where crisp 'hard-edge' effects are sought, it will be found that acrylics will tend to handle more easily than watercolour gouache, and also where it is necessary to have a large area of flat even-toned opaque colour, once again the acrylics will produce the desired result in a simpler manner.

A combination of wash and opaque methods can produce a great many exciting and subtle effects. Opaque colour can be applied over a previously laid wash and scumbled whilst moist; for example, white woolly clouds can have their edges broken and softened, either by teasing with a bristle brush or by gently rubbing with a finger tip. Here can be appreciated some of the advantages of the speed of drying, as in some cases this may be only a few minutes. This allows for far less waste of time; overlays and glazes and further coats can be put on very quickly whilst the inspiration is fresh.

One of the most engaging and fascinating methods in painting is that of glazing. It was briefly mentioned in the section on washes. Here a painter, understanding what the transparent qualities of particular colours will realize, deliberately leaves areas of his picture to be completed later by the application of layers of glaze. This means simply that some colours, like alizarin crimson, are very largely transparent and when mixed with water or water and acrylic medium can be laid over so that the areas are given a gentle veil of the particular tint. Titian, the great Venetian master, employed the manner to good results, knowing how it can add a great sense of richness and translucence to particular areas of a picture. He would, of course, have been working in oils, which would have meant that he might have had to wait several weeks before he could apply the glaze over the areas of earlier paint. With acrylics this wait may be only a matter of a few minutes or at the most an hour or so; this allows for a far greater freedom of choice in glazing methods.

The choice of brush for opaque application may be anything between a tiny round soft-hair for picking out small details or crisp edges up to large hog-bristle. For blending large areas it is simpler to use as large a brush as practical and to get the colour on with broad sweeping strokes.

Sometimes it is an advantage to use a flat opaque under-painting of the scene or composition for the final heavier paint to come. In its simplest form, this early layer could be an absolutely flat monochrome or 'imprimatura' of a warm tone of burnt umber or burnt umber and yellow ochre. Into this the main masses of the composition can then be laid in their relatively correct tones.

Impasto

One of the dangers when working with oils or gouache is that if the colours are applied too thickly, they will not dry out properly and can crack or flake away. A great many painters of this century have used an increasingly thick impasto and in some cases this has already led to damage. Here is one of the outstanding advantages for acrylic paints, that they can be applied really very thickly and will still dry out quite safely. What causes the trouble with oil colours when thick is that the oil takes a very long time to dry out and particularly if it has been applied in several layers at intervals; the different speeds of drying out between the films causing cracking. With gouache, heavy paint does not really have enough binder to hold down considerable thicknesses of the dry paint. With acrylic, as the vehicle itself is a strong adhesive and as it dries out very quickly, after about an hour or so there is no further movement in the paint film and the whole is locked firmly in place.

With the application of impasto in the building up of texture, brush-work is all important, and also so is the working quality of the paint itself. As strokes will be placed close to one another, even touching, and at times through one another, a paint that will not bleed is of great advantage. It will be found, with using acrylics, that wet beside wet and even wet through wet can be achieved so that the fullest sparkle and cleanliness of the individual colours is retained. Here again the speed of drying assists, as in difficult passages the picture only needs to be left for about an hour before it can be worked on anew and fresh layers of colour be applied.

One point worth experimenting with for heavy impasto or texture work is the bulking of colours. This may be done to increase the stiffness by adding amounts of kaolin, marble dust or whiting. It will be found that in general the brightness and the strength of the colours will not be largely affected if the addition is not more than a quarter by bulk. If economy is necessary the colours

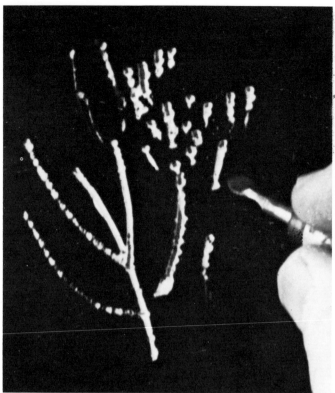 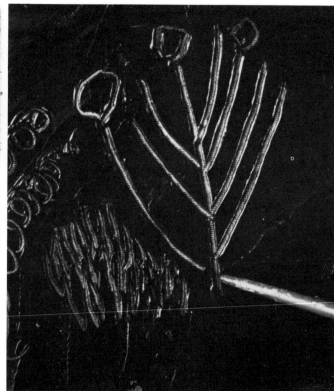

Left. Where the paint has been laid on to a gesso panel effective sgraffito can be worked up with the use of a sharp tool such as a scraper-board knife.

Right. Scraping into wet paint with the end of a brush handle.

can be bulked further by the addition of decorators' powder colours, which have a fairly low tinting power. When this is done it can be possible to add up to half the bulk depending upon the particular colour. It will also be necessary to add some acrylic medium to get the consistency of paint needed.

Sgraffito

To obtain the maximum effect with sgraffito, or scratching through, the picture should be painted on a gesso panel. Such a panel can be prepared in the following way.

An ounce of rabbit-skin glue should be left to soak overnight in a pint of water. The next morning it should be heated in a double boiler or glue-pot until it has dissolved, although care should be taken that the glue does not boil for this will affect the binding qualities. When the rabbit-skin glue has completely dissolved, stir in enough whiting, kaolin or marble dust to produce a fairly thick cream. It is important that this stirring is done thoroughly and that there are no lumps left. A final precaution can be to strain the gesso through an old nylon stocking, the resulting creamy mixture can be applied to a piece of hardboard or wood panel by a brush or felt-covered roller. When this has hardened, it may be smoothed down with sandpaper. For the best effect of all, a second coat of milk-thin gesso can be applied and the resulting surface should, after about forty-eight hours, be as smooth and hard as ivory.

The idea of sgraffito is that the picture can be, to a certain extent, painted in the normal manner with thick or thin colours, and then where particular accents or extra textural effects are called for, these can be achieved by scraping through the colour to expose the white gesso underneath; the scraping through can be done using knife blades, razor blades, scraper-board tools, steel wool, sand-paper and other abrasive instruments or substances.

Another variation of this manner and one that can lend itself to very unusual treatments is to put down different coloured layers of gesso. To do this, it is better to make the gesso using acrylic medium and acrylic colours; for example, a layer of yellow gesso could be laid, on top of this when it is dry a layer of black, and thereafter a layer of blue, and another of red. When a scraping tool is now used it will be possible to expose one or more of the underlying colours, which will allow for unusual textural and colour effects not obtainable by any other method, and into all this various types of painting can be carried out as the work progresses. Obviously with sgraffito methods and especially this second method, the picture has to be carefully planned in advance, as once a cutting into the gesso has been made it is impossible to correct.

Glass painting

This is a technique which had a fashion in the last century, especially on the Continent and in America, and which is today having some revival. The method really involves painting backwards, in that to achieve a composition the final

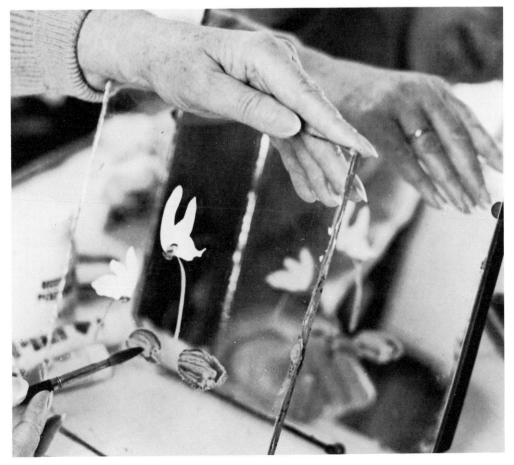

An aid in back-glass painting can be use of a mirror. With this technique one has to work, to a degree, backwards; highlights and everything in the foreground having to go in first. If one can rig up a mirror, as here, behind the glass panel, it will be of great assistance.

strokes have to be put on first and background colours placed last. First of all, the piece of glass to be used should be thoroughly degreased by wiping over with a piece of cotton wool dipped in methylated spirits. After the methylated spirits have evaporated, the painting with acrylics can begin, using the colour fairly stiff – if it is too diluted it will run and be difficult to control on the glass. When the picture has been completed, the whole of the back of the paint surface should be given one or two coats of mat medium to bind the surface together.

Action painting

The method of applying colour in a somewhat unconscious and uncontrolled manner was given popularity by the American painter Jackson Pollock. His canvases are recognisable by a haphazard dribbling, splashing and spotting of the paints on to the support. Acrylic colours, with their speed of drying, are eminently suitable for this method of picture-making. First one layer, and then another can be applied; the colours can be manipulated by tilting the support so that they run; by movement with brushes; by scraping with different tools; and if it is suddenly necessary to get a particular area to stop bleeding or smudging, the drying speed of the colours can be greatly accelerated by the use of a hot-air blower, a hair-drier, an electric fan, or local heat. Action painting is best done with the support lying flat on the floor.

Below. Steps in building a collage. (1) One of the easiest procedures can be to use acrylic paints, as they are strong adhesives in themselves. The colours can be put on quite thickly and freely and then the materials pressed into them.

(2) More paint, more materials. Corrugated paper, textiles.

(3) Almost any materials will stick firmly in this way. Feathers, fur, wool, tissue paper and wheat heads. When complete the collage should be left flat to harden for about twenty-four hours. Very fragile materials can be strengthened by lightly spraying them with a mixture of one part acrylic medium and two parts water.

Collage

One of the most exciting methods of visual expression that has risen to popularity in this century has been collage. Although it does not consist entirely of painting, it is included here as the acrylic colours are ideally suited for use with this method. One of the principal drawbacks of collage before the introduction of acrylics was that these pictures were often built up with a thoroughly unstable mixture of media, adhesives and materials. Examples can be seen in galleries and collections where the materials have faded, paint films have cracked and adhesives have given way.

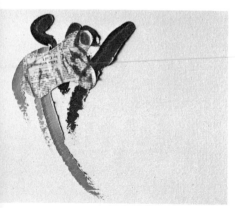
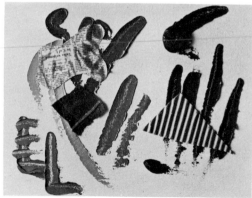
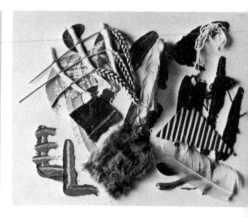

The principle of collage is to introduce into painting techniques the use of other materials such as heavy textiles, newspaper, cardboard, cork, wood shavings, string, gravel, to so produce contrast not only of texture and colour, but also a degree of third dimensional effect.

As the acrylic colours themselves are a powerful adhesive, they are very suitable for collage because thick paint can be applied and into this the other various materials can be pressed. It is important, as far as possible, to avoid substances that will change with time such as newspaper, which will go brown. If it is desired to incorporate in the collage a number of fragile objects like crumpled pieces of tissue or thin wood shavings, these can be consolidated and given further strength by spraying with a mixture of half water and half acrylic medium.

The support for a collage should be at least a stiff card, as the weight of material would very soon cause even strong paper to buckle. It is better to use a piece of hardboard, probably this time working on the rough side which will provide more opportunity for adhesion.

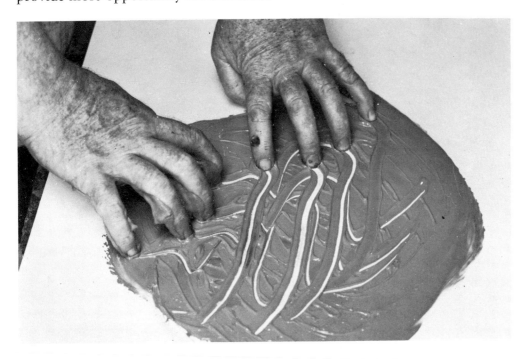

Finger painting can be a useful exercise in directness. The two most important points are to have plenty of thick creamy colour and a fairly non-absorbent paper or card on which to work.

Blot and finger painting

The first of these is closely allied to action painting, as to a certain extent the effect is not controlled. The colours can be placed to a set pattern or design, or haphazardly, and then blotted with a second sheet of paper. The effect will vary according to the consistency of the colour, more or less acrylic medium being added as desired.

Finger painting was originally an Oriental technique and allows for the creation of unusual effects by rhythmic movements of the fingers and hand. It is best carried out on a glossy or hot-pressed, non-absorbent paper; the colours should be put on to the paper at the consistency they come out of the tube and then manipulated as wished. Although not strictly a painting technique, finger painting and blotting can be used in conjunction with other painting techniques.

Monotype

A method for producing a single print, which relies on painting for its reproduction rather than etching, engraving or cutting. For a monotype a sheet of clean glass, formica or metal is needed. On to this the picture to be reproduced can be painted with acrylics using thin and thick applications, sgraffito, scraped and scumbled colours. Then, when the design is complete, a sheet of mulberry tissue or thin cartridge is placed over the surface and gently pressed with the palm of the hand, and then lifted off. Often the results can be exciting and unpredictable; much of this is a happy accident, although with practice a degree of control is possible. It is important to remember that the laying-in of the picture must be done quickly owing to the drying speed of the acrylics.

Alkyd colours

Oil painting has attracted the great majority of artists since the fourteenth century. Yet, despite the brilliance and richness of the colours when using oil as a vehicle, painters have been conscious of the restrictions of the medium. Acrylic paints have, for many, afforded a freedom, but at the same time the painter who appreciates the qualities of oil colours does not seem to find in them all he desires.

Recently, however, scientists have made a 'breakthrough' by discovering that paints using an alkyd resin as the vehicle make available to the artist a range

Left. Producing a monotype print can often provide an idea from which a painting may be worked up. All that is needed is a sheet of glass, plastic or metal. On this the colour should be liberally applied, either with brushes or straight from the tube.

Right. Then a sheet of paper is laid on top of the wet paint and pressed down lightly and smoothly with the palm of the hand. After this it can be gently peeled off.

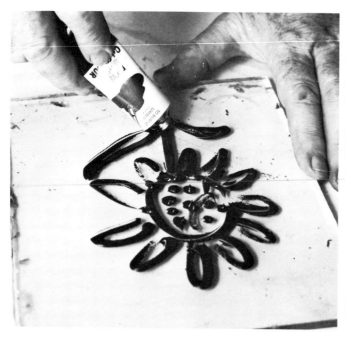

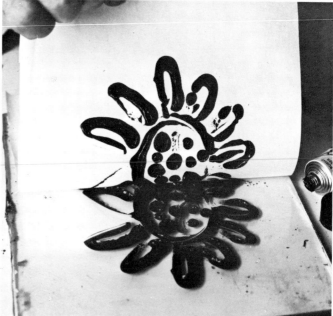

of colours which allows for all the oil techniques whilst simultaneously removing most of the undesirable risks or side effects.

In 1927 a substance produced from alcohols and acids went under the name of 'Alcid', a title coined by Kienle. From this name comes today's term of Alkyd, and from the extensive range of these alkyd resins, one has been selected as promising the greatest possibilities in variety of handling when mixed with pigments. The alkyd colours are produced to be used in the same manner as oils, and it will be found that this is just what can be done with them. With a number of methods they will handle better and yield more impressive results.

Brushes of all types of bristle, hair and synthetic fibres may be used, with the same precautions for cleaning after painting. Rinse well with white spirit or turpentine substitute, and then wash out with warm water and soap, carefully shaping the heads before leaving to dry.

Wooden oil palettes are quite suitable, also tear-off greaseproof paper, sheets of heavy gauge glass and ceramic tiles. Enamelled metal palettes are not advisable owing to the high degree of adherence of these colours – in cleaning it is likely the enamel could be lifted off.

All the supports used with oils apply to this medium. These include acrylic-primed and oil-primed flax and cotton canvas, canvas boards, prepared boards, metal surfaces (if they have been de-greased with methylated spirit), and also glass (if it has been similarly treated). Heavy papers or cards, which may be satisfactory for small sketches, should always be given some form of priming first.

The principal difference in the 'feel' of alkyds from that of oils is that the brushing quality has slightly more drag in it. But this is a small point compared with the considerable gains. It will be found, for instance, that all pigments when ground in alkyd resin have a uniformity of consistency and a controlled drying time; the colours skin-drying in eighteen hours.

Should greater fluidity be desired, it can be achieved by mixing in small quantities of white spirit. Water must not be mixed with alkyds as it can be with acrylics. It is all right to apply oil colours over previously laid and dried alkyds, but not the other way round, owing to the wide diversity of drying out time for the different oil colours.

If old oil painting manuals from past centuries are examined, it will be noted how many artists have attempted from time to time to improve the nature of oil colours by mixing in with them some strange additives; these have included waxes, exotic oils and emulsions. Seldom have these experiments been successful; generally resulting in fugitive qualities such as darkening, cracking, rivelling and desiccation of the paint film.

The grinding of pigments into an alkyd resin has produced a paint that is non-yellowing and also remarkably resistant to environmental atmosphere.

On drying out it achieves a satisfactorily uniform surface over all the colours, and one which when of normal thickness can be covered with similar varnishes to those used on oils; and after only a month instead of a year.

The consistency of the paints faithfully retains the brush and bristle marks. In the same way knife-painting is facilitated, and clean distinct strokes are obtained. Direct painting in one sitting can be more easily carried out, as the alkyd colours have very little tendency to bleed. Wet strokes can be placed touching and even taken right through each other. For glazing, alkyds will be found to produce effects that would be more or less impossible with oils. When the paints are diluted right down to wash consistency with white spirit or turpentine substitute they will handle in a very controlled manner. There is complete fluidity in application, combined with blending and bleeding when desired. A number of effects can be produced ranging from the palest 'carnation' to the near opaque, depending on the dilution. They can be blotted and wiped with clean rag or cotton wool.

To sum up the alkyds, it is best to think of them as a considerable extension to oils; being able to achieve everything that the older medium can, but at the same time allowing more freedom, and making safer many of the technique manners of the past.

Watercolour and gouache

Watercolour, apart from the early cave drawings, the exact technique of which is not certain, is the oldest method of painting. The basic difference between watercolour and gouache is that the term watercolour means in its purest sense painting with transparent colours, and gouache is when body or opaque colours are used. Under these headings in their broadest sense come poster colour, showcard, distemper and powder colour. The pigments are bound with an aqueous solution of a gum or glue. The use of watercolour and gouache has spread all over the world. The most exquisite examples of purist technique have come perhaps from the Chinese and the Japanese. The wonderful illuminated manuscripts produced at places like Kells and Lindisfarne were decorated with forms of watercolour and gouache by the monks. Although watercolour and gouache can be used in conjunction with pastels, crayons, charcoal and inks in mixed media pictures, this practice should be done with care to avoid impermanence. In general use, both these methods should employ water only as a diluent and on no account should oil, spirits, or acrylics be mixed with them; for if this happens their own particular working characteristics will be changed.

Watercolour and gouache can be used on cartridge, handmade rag papers, also on pasteless boards and specially prepared cards. The surface does not need any special priming or grounding; all that is necessary with papers that are not stretched is to lightly sponge over the surface with water to remove any surplus size and dust. If however the paper to be painted on is cartridge or fairly lightweight rag, it does need to be stretched to prevent the paper buckling when large amounts of colour are being used. The stretching is done on to a drawing-board. First of all, the right side of the paper should be ascertained; if it is not possible to do this by seeing a milling mark on the back, the paper can be held up to the light and the watermark read – normally the side from which it

Below. Stretching paper.
(1) To prevent paper buckling when working with water-based media, it should be first stretched. Stage one is to soak the back of the paper using a soft sponge that will not damage the surface.

(2) Turn the paper over. Wet the front, and then by lifting one corner and then the others, smooth the wrinkles and bubbles out until the sheet lies quite flat.

(3) Moisten strips of adhesive paper tape and smooth them into position round the edges of the sheet.

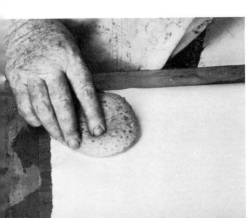
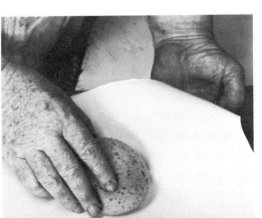
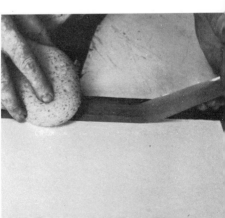

can be read the right way round is the front of the paper. The paper is then laid face down on the drawing-board and the back is amply moistened with a sponge and water. It is then turned over and laid square on the board so that there is at least an inch of wood showing all the way round. The front is now moistened and as the whole paper starts to buckle, one corner after another is lifted and the paper is smoothed flat with the wet sponge. After all the buckling has ceased and the paper is quite flat the edges are stuck to the drawing-board with lengths of sticky tape. When the paper dries out it will be drumhead tight and will not move even with the heaviest washes. Although stretching is a rather protracted business, it is well worth doing, for if washes are attempted over buckled paper uneven areas of colour are liable to gather in the valleys.

The brushes for watercolour are largely a matter of economics. Undoubtedly the most expensive are the best and over the years will probably come out cheapest. A good watercolour brush is made of sable and should hold its colour well, and the round ones should come to a point and hold their shape. The cheaper versions are made from ox hair, squirrel, ringcat, pony and other animal hair. Of these the most reliable and the best are those from ox hair.

The palette for watercolour can be anything from an old chipped and cracked dinner plate or plastic cream cup to one of the expensive glazed porcelain examples. Although the specially-made palettes are probably more convenient, there is not a great deal of real practical advantage. As long as the container chosen will hold water and will allow for adequate mixing, almost anything will do.

Watercolours can be purchased in small porcelain or plastic pans, in cakes, in tubes, in pots, and in sticks. As to which is bought, it will depend very largely on the method of painting. Probably in many ways a combination of tubes and pans is the most practical. Some makers put out a range of colours under the heading of designers' gouache and these are perfectly suitable for use in conjunction with watercolours to provide body and heavier paint when necessary. Watercolours in stick form are generally used by architects and draughtsmen but they are useful for giving delicate washes.

The range of watercolour techniques is various: from the delicate transparent washes of the eighteenth-century English watercolourists to the broadest fiery, almost impasto, treatment of some practitioners today. One feature, however, applies to any method and that is, that the composition should be worked out carefully before a start is made, as if the full freshness of watercolour is to be attained, it is almost impossible to make corrections. To a certain extent, this also applies to gouache, although with the heavier opaque body colours it is possible to overpaint and hide an error.

As with acrylics, the best way to do the preliminary work is to draw in with a brush, using a weak neutral tone. If this is kept very light, as the work proceeds and the main features are established, these first strokes will all but disappear.

Looking back at the master performers with watercolours does help the beginner, as almost all of the great names had their own particular manner which was worked out and polished for their own use. Some idea of the effects possible can be glimpsed. Paul Sandby had to a large extent the draughtsman's approach, with areas of colour being secondary to a careful drawing. Cozens and Cotman employed a far greater freedom. Cox and Girtin did much to comfort aspiring followers with the use of broad free brush-work and the employing of heavy body colours. Many of the leading watercolourists today use a variety of tricks from isolation and wax to erasers, sandpaper and knife blades. Tinted and grained papers have become popular. What it all really adds up to is that in the last estimate it does not matter what methods have been used, it is the picture that will be judged. This does not mean to say that it is not necessary to have an understanding of the ways in which watercolour and gouache can be used; this knowledge is essential if full freedom is to be gained.

When setting out the table for watercolour and gouache, allow plenty of room for not only the board but also paints, palettes, several jars of clean water, clean cotton rags, and space for brushes. If everything that you need is laid out in a known ordered manner, it will save time as you paint.

Although watercolour is one of the simplest of the painting methods, in that it does not have oils, varnishes and additives, it is a method that needs understanding, directness and practice to succeed. Therefore, if certain exercises in the handling of the colours can be carried out, this will save much frustration at a later date. Although highly dramatic effects can be obtained with watercolour, it has to be handled with delicacy and the constant realization that mistakes are almost impossible to remedy.

It is only occasionally that completely flat colour washes are called for, but it is just as well to practise the putting on of these. The first essential is to have sufficient colour mixed before the start is made and, if it is a colour with a heavy pigment, to keep the wash well stirred each time you pick up the colour with the brush. The board should be slightly tilted and a well-loaded brush should be taken from left to right across the top. Then re-load the brush and repeat from left to right, sweeping the brush gently through the weight of colour as it descends. As far as possible, try to avoid leaving any missed spaces, as if you start going back on a wash it is almost certain that the continuous even tone will be spoilt. Never scrub the colour on, going backwards and forwards with a heavy hand, as again the result will be spoilt. When the full area has been covered, allow the weight of colour to run to the bottom and then gently lift off the excess with a dry brush or blotting paper, but be careful that you do not over-dry or there will be an unpleasant light tone at the bottom. That is basically the system for putting on a flat wash; from this you can work on to graded washes, wiping out and bleeding in other colours.

Graded washes, either going from dark to light or changing from one colour to another, are worth practising. The simplest, going from dark to light or the other way, can be carried out in a similar manner to the description of the process in *Acrylics* page 28. It should be remembered that pure watercolour will

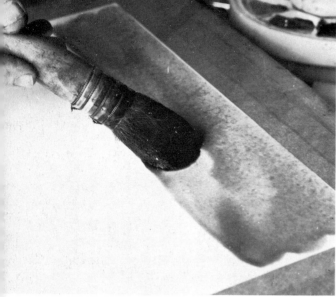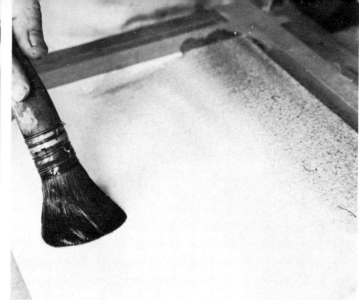

Left. To lay a wash, use the largest convenient brush or mop. Have the board sloping at an angle of about ten degrees. Don't scrub the colour down the sheet, rather let the weight of the wash carry it down gently assisted by caressing strokes. Always have plenty of colour mixed up, because you cannot stop in the middle to mix up fresh supplies.

Right. To grade out the colour from a wash, have plenty of clean water available. As the wash goes down the sheet go on adding more and more clean water until the colour disappears quite evenly.

react in a more gentle manner and will flow more quickly than with acrylics. If, for example, in the first instance a plain blue sky is to be graded down to nearly white, the easiest way is to prepare three washes of dark, medium and light blue and have an ample supply of clean water. Start at the top with two or three strokes of the *dark* blue, then dip your brush into the *medium* blue and put in two or three more strokes. Follow this with similar treatment with the *light* blue and lastly with clean water. It may take some time to learn the trick of doing this so that the final effect is not striped, but perseverance will bring success. When it is desired to blend two colours, for example, a blue sky changing to an orange sunset, the procedure is to mix up two or three shades of blue and two or three shades of orange. Starting at the top, as before with the blue, gradually lose its strength; at the meeting point use clear water and then bring in the orange and intensify as the wash proceeds. Once a graded wash has been laid, it is best to leave it lying flat to dry.

Wiping out in a wash is done in a very similar manner to that described with acrylics. It should be emphasized here that as far as possible when removing areas with a wet brush, use as delicate a touch as possible and never scrub heavily with the brush as this is liable to disturb the texture of the paper and leave an unsightly mark. One of the best things for taking out a cloud or a light area from a freshly laid wash is a piece of soft good-quality natural sponge; this will lift a lot of moisture but will be unlikely to damage the paper. Clean white blotting paper or clean white cotton rag can also be used.

If it is desired to 'bleed' other colours wet into wet, it will be found that pure watercolour reacts much more freely to this treatment than acrylics. To do this, the board should be laid flat and the attempt should be made whilst the wash is still fresh and very wet. A brush well filled, for example with purple-grey for clouds, can gently touch the wet surface to simulate a cloud shape. As soon as the colour starts to 'bleed' very little can be done to control the spread; to a certain degree judicious tipping of the board may be used and blotting with a sponge, but largely the result will depend at first on 'happy accident'.

Watercolour painting is in many ways a medium of speed. Thus, as men-

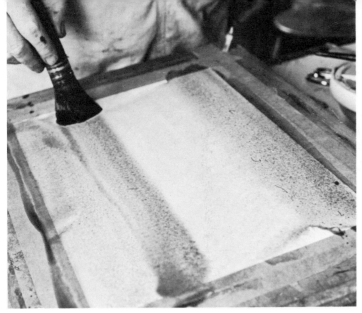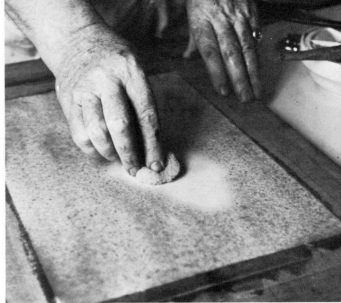

tioned earlier, an organised array of materials is necessary so that the hand can automatically go to the brush, colour or the pot. Pan or cake colours can have a drop of water put on them at the start, in order that the colour will lift quickly when the time comes. The more spare palettes available the better, as a lot of area is needed for mixing watercolours, and to maintain their purity a clean space is really needed each time.

Right from the start, try to get used to working with the largest brush that will make the strokes and marks needed. Generally speaking, the broader, in the mass, that a watercolour is kept the more successful the result will be. If you are to paint freely, a certain waste of colour must be expected. It is essential to use as far as possible fresh, clean colours or mixes each time. Muddy, dirty colours are more noticeable with watercolour than any other medium. Never use a dirty brush on fresh colour squeezed from a tube or on fresh colour in a pan or a cake. Get into the habit of rinsing and cleaning the brushes constantly.

In pure watercolour, to a large degree you are working with transparent paints. Much of the effect comes from the white or tinted paper showing through the colours. Even when other colours are superimposed, still this transparency must be borne in mind; although the techniques of blotting and wiping out have been discussed, the purist likes to leave areas of untouched paper showing through for highlights and sparkle.

Left. To successfully introduce a second or third colour into a wash the application should be made as quickly as possible; if areas start to dry off the result will very soon become uneven.

Right. Light areas for clouds or other purposes can be sponged out.

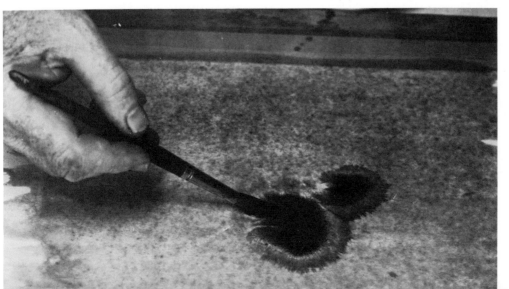

Often exciting and unusual effects can be obtained by dropping strong colour into a wet wash.

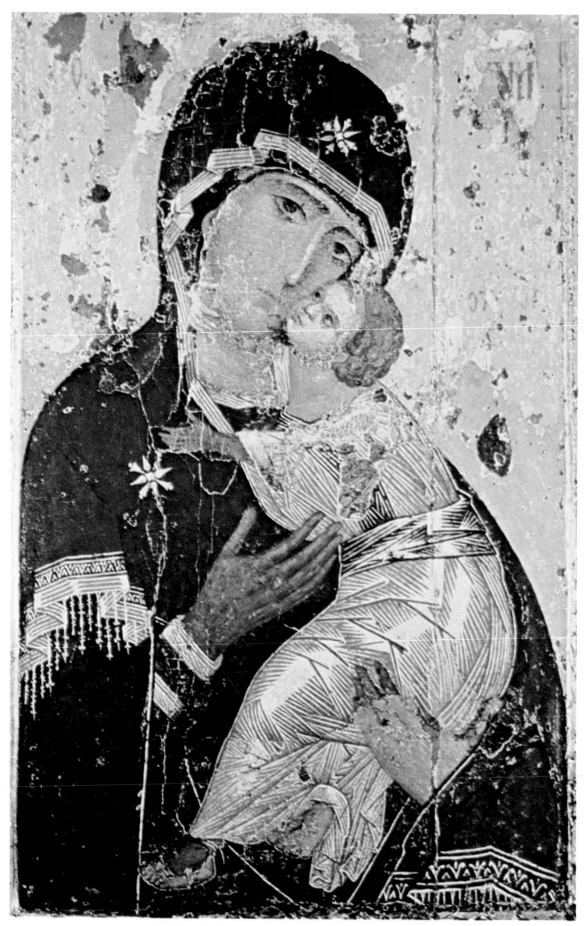

The **Virgin** of Vladimir (*c* 1125) *Tretyakov Gallery, Moscow*

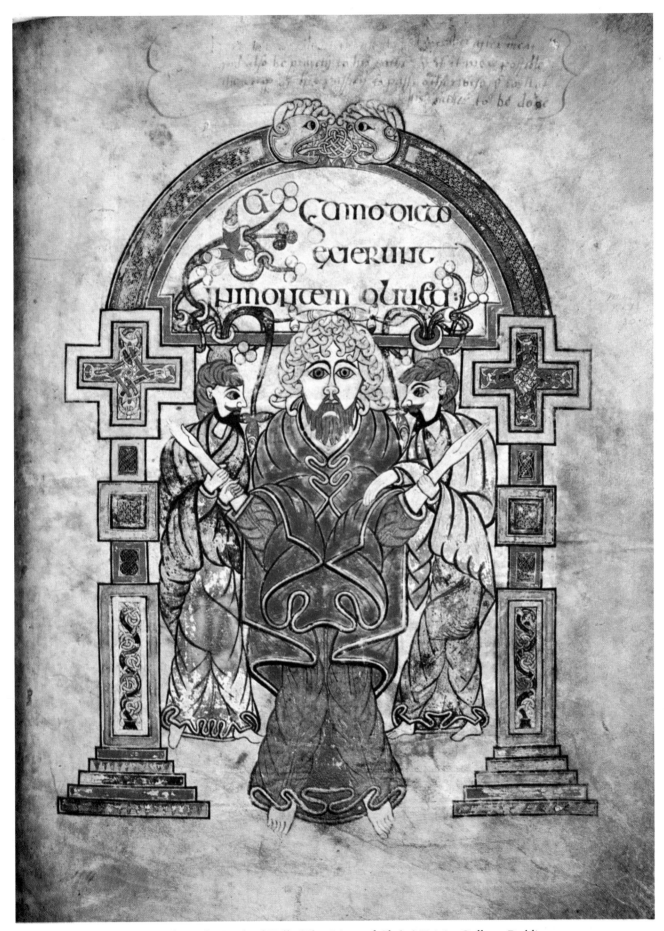

A page from the Book of Kells 'The Arrest of Christ' *Trinity College, Dublin*

Gouache

This term, which in its general sense means the use of body or opaque colours with watercolour, describes a technique that lies half way between pure watercolour and oil or acrylic methods. In its simplest sense gouache implies the use of a white opaque pigment such as Chinese white; this being mixed with the other colours gives them a body and they lose their transparency, thus overpainting is possible and brush-work becomes important. With watercolour by itself brush-strokes are used to guide the colour, but do not place it in the same way as with the application of opaque colours, where each stroke can become part of the subject. When a whole range of gouache tubed colours is used it is important not to be carried away so as to start building up heavy impasto, as with acrylics or oils, because these lightly glue-bound colours have not the ability to withstand cracking and pieces of colour can easily flake away. A combination of watercolour and gouache is probably better than an overall picture in gouache which can be difficult to control, and may also lose much of its freshness and power with too much overpainting. It is possible to varnish or wax a gouache, but an experiment should be made first on a piece of paper which has the same colours, as these may darken in tone when treated. The most suitable type of varnish is a thin synthetic resin, which should be applied with a wide soft brush, care being taken that the film is even. If the picture is to be waxed, this can be done using a beeswax polish on a small piece of cotton wool. The wax should be applied sparingly; the picture should be left for about half-an-hour, and then the surface gently buffed up.

ABRASION

If a close examination is made of some of the watercolours of, for example, Turner, it can be seen how he at times scratched and cut into his paper to produce highlights. If the picture has been painted on very thick rag paper, it is quite possible, using a razor blade, to cut out a tiny V-sectioned strip to

Below left. Light rays can be imitated by using a soft eraser gently rubbed across the colour.

Centre. When working on thicker paper it is possible to use sand-paper to achieve scratch effects.

Right. When working on very heavy rag paper, pasteless boards or card, highlights can be cut out in the form of shallow trenches, using a scalpel.

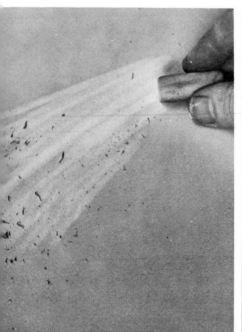
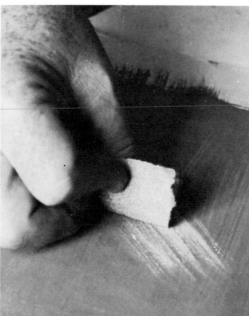
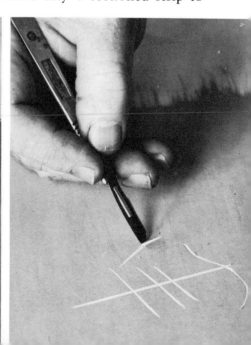

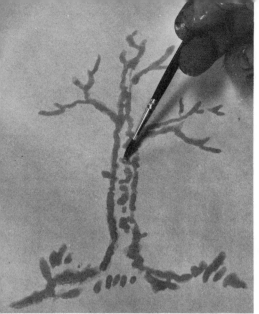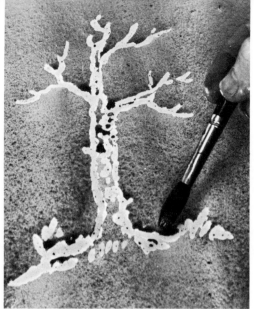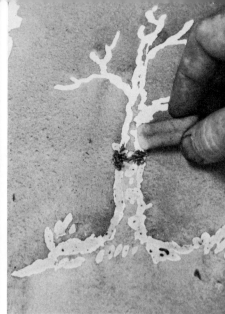

represent the edge of a piece of glass or sunlight catching a piece of wet wire. This sudden exposing of the pure white paper can be used with dramatic effect, but it is a trick which should be employed only sparingly.

Similarly the white paper can be exposed to give textural effects by scraping with a razor blade or knife or by rubbing with different grades of sandpaper.

Gentler abrasive effects can be achieved on pure watercolour by the use of an eraser; for example, sunlight streaming through a window. To get the edge desired, a ruler or piece of stiff card can be held in position whilst the eraser is being used. Obviously it is important that the picture should be quite dry before this method is applied or the paper will very quickly be torn.

ISOLATION

Sometimes it is very difficult to preserve areas of white paper during the painting. To a certain extent this can be done, before painting, by placing in position pieces of masking tape. This is not always easy to do and there is always a danger the colour will 'bleed' under it, or that when it is removed the tape will damage the paper. A much better course is to use a latex rubber adhesive. This can be lightly brushed over the areas to be left white. When the colour washes have dried the latex adhesive can be easily removed with a piece of soft art gum.

Using masking fluid. (1) A device for isolating an area when applying a wash background is to use a 'masking fluid'. The parts of the picture to be kept white should be freely painted with the fluid.

(2) When the fluid has hardened the wash is applied. Large blobs of colour trapped by the hardened masking fluid should be lifted out with a brush or a piece of blotting paper.

(3) After the wash has dried the hardened masking fluid can be pulled off with a soft eraser.

Mixed media

It is possible to combine other techniques with watercolour and gouache, and a wide variety of interesting and lively effects can thus be produced.

Pastel can be combined with gouache in one of two ways. A pastel drawing can be prepared and after it has been thoroughly fixed, gouache may be applied on the top. It is important to make certain that all the loose grains of pastel pigment have been thoroughly fixed or shaken off as if they mix with the gouache

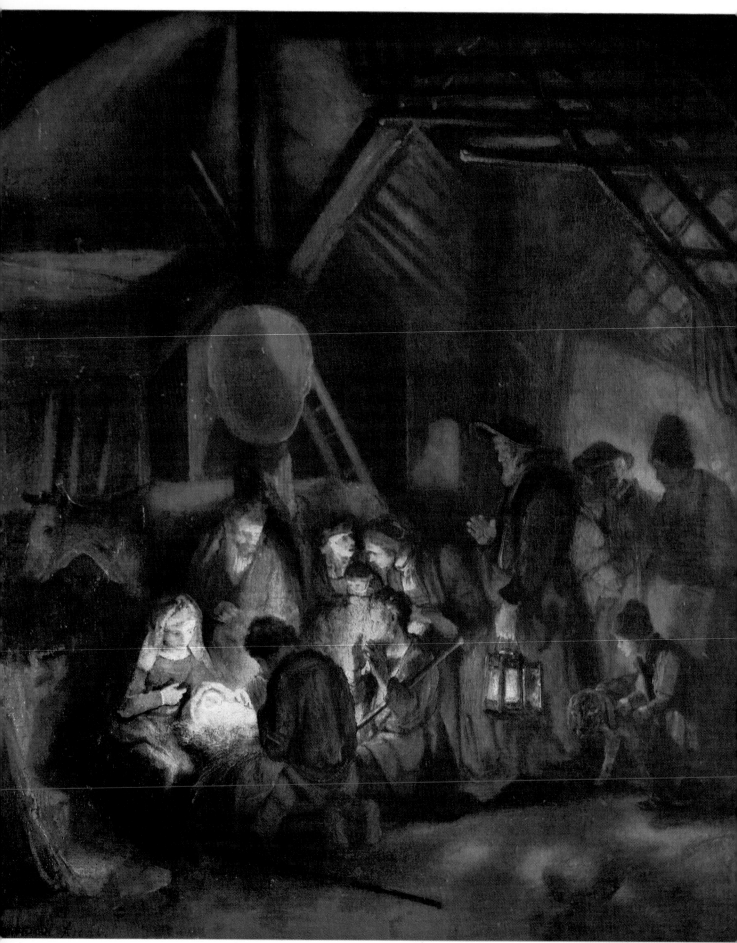

Rembrandt: The Adoration of the Shepherds 655 × 550 mm *The National Gallery, London*

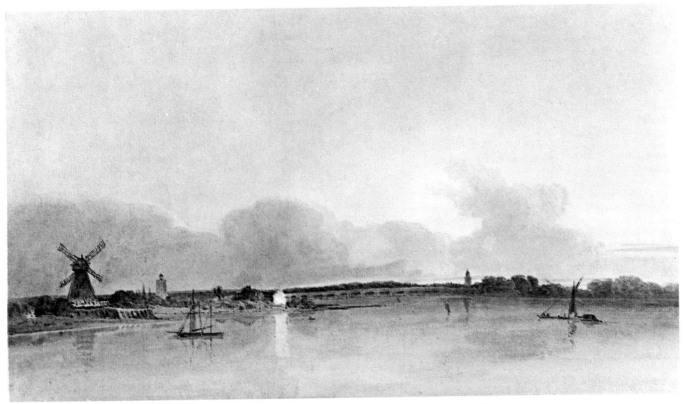

Girtin: The White House, Chelsea (Watercolour) 298 × 514 mm *Tate Gallery, London* (page 47)

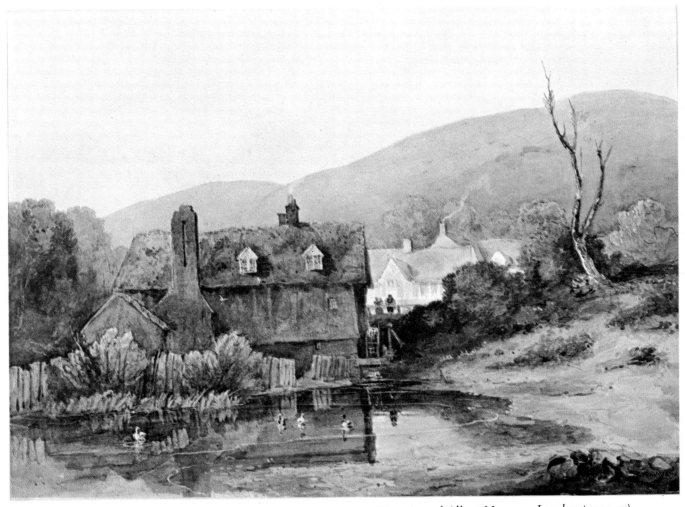

Cox: Watermill in North Wales (Gouache) 375 × 525 mm *Victoria and Albert Museum, London* (page 47)

colours they will bring them down in tone and lose some of their life.

Pastel may also be put on top of gouache, provided the paint is not too thick. If pastel is used in this way it should be applied with direct strokes and not manipulated afterwards by rubbing with a paper-stump or finger tip. After the picture is finished the pastel will have to be fixed. But as the fixative may affect the tone values of the gouache, tests should really be made on scrap pieces of paper before beginning.

Pastel can also be used on pure watercolour. The watercolour can be carried out rather in the manner of underpainting, leaving the accents and strengths to be put in with the pastel.

Pen and ink is often combined with watercolour and the sharp ink lines can produce a pleasant contrast. There is a wide variety of pen nibs ranging from the finest mapping pens to broad pens that can be cut from reeds and bamboos. It is best to wait until the watercolour is dry before drawing in, as the Indian ink bleeding into wet colours will not produce a desirable effect in the same manner as watercolours.

WAX RESIST

To achieve broken and speckled effects with areas of watercolour or light gouache, the paper can be rubbed with a piece of wax candle. The intensity of the effect will vary with the amount of wax that is applied and also the strength of tone of the overlaid colours. Wax resist can be repeated over and over again in different areas and on top of succeeding layers of colour. Interesting effects can also be achieved by the use of coloured wax crayons.

Left. Speckled and irregular effects with watercolour can be obtained by the use of 'wax resist'. The surface to be worked on should be liberally rubbed with a normal wax candle.

Right. Then the colour can be brushed over the waxed surface. Care should be taken that the consistency of the paint is not too thick or it will not break over the wax.

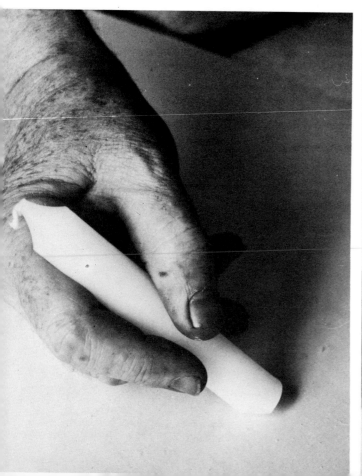

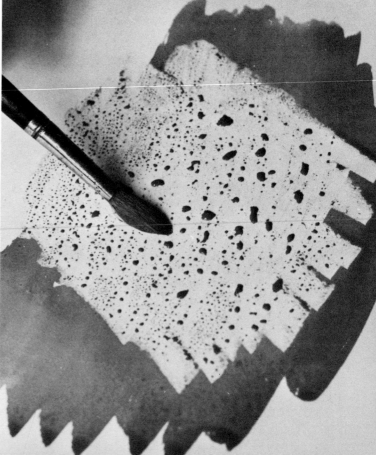

Oil painting

During the past five hundred years practically every major picture has been painted in oils. Despite the fact that the other techniques may have some advantages in application and in method and preparation, oil painting holds pride of place with the great majority of artists. The reasons for this are that no other medium can bring out the full richness of the colours nor provide such enjoyable painting qualities and variety of finishes. Watercolour may have its delicacy and its spontaneity; acrylics may have their rugged and versatile characteristics; tempera may possess subtle varieties of tone and tint; but with none of these are the glorious colour possibilities realized as with oils. Whether it is for the beginner or the practised painter, there is something about squeezing out the colours on to the palette, the smell of the oils drifting up the nostrils, and sensing the feel of the brush or knife in the buttery paint that evokes a sense of inspiration before even a start is made.

The discovery of oil painting was not an overnight flash, rather was it an evolution. The early artists of the thirteenth century in Italy and other places worked in fresco, the art of painting on moist plaster with the colours mixed with lime water, and tempera, where the pigments are ground with egg yolk. Both these media have technical disadvantages, and in both cases the palette is limited and the pigments that are used are seldom bright or high in tinting power. Painters, possibly from the school of Venice, must gradually have begun experimenting by grinding the pigments in oil, and they found that at once these same pigments had a new astonishing richness and translucence; also that this new medium had great flexibility in use; the colours could be manipulated with great freedom; and there were many ways of application. The credit for the perfecting of oil painting can probably be given to those two Flemish painters Hubert and Jan Van Eyck. A study of *Giovanni Arnolfini and His Wife* by Jan Van Eyck in the National Gallery, painted in 1334 at Bruges, illustrates the great advance of this medium and how it was exploited to the full by the painter. You will see how rich the colours are and how the artist has been able to enjoy himself to the full with the rendering of textures and fine details.

One of the main releases that oils can give the artist is freedom to use long sweeping strokes, while allowing for the maximum of textural and transparent effects without the loss of colour brilliance – which is liable to happen when

Oil colours

From left to right: French
Ultramarine, Monastral
Blue, Burnt Umber, Raw
Umber. At the top pure
colours, and below mixtures
with the same but varying
amounts of white. Note how
some colours appear to alter
characteristics.

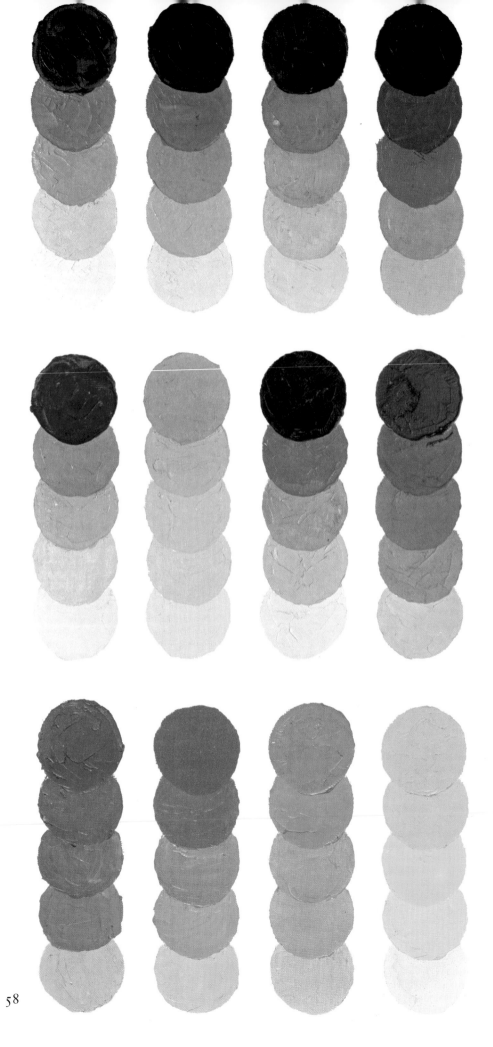

From left to right: Viridian,
Cadmium Green, Violet
Alizarin, Magenta. At the
top pure colours, and below
mixtures with the same but
varying amounts of white.
Note how some colours
appear to alter characteristics.

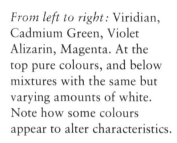

From left to right: Indian
Red, Cadmium Red, Yellow
Ochre, Cadmium Yellow.
At the top pure colours, and
below mixtures with the same
but varying amounts of
White. Note how some
colours appear to alter
characteristics.

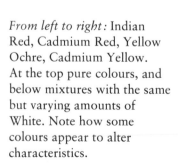

58

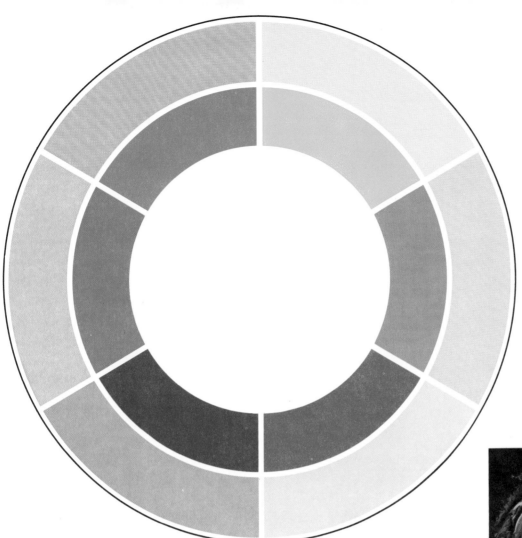

Colour circle
The inner circle shows colours and mixes at full strength. The outer circle with additions of White.

Close-up of mix
Try to be as direct as possible; better to have some separation showing than to 'puddle' away until all that is left is mud.

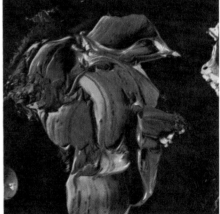

Mixing oil colours

1. **Palette loaded** Place the colours well towards the edge of the palette so as to leave plenty of space in which to carry out the mixing. It is a good practice to establish a fixed order for yourself and stay with it.

2. **Palette with mixes** When mixing pull the pure colours away from the main piles.

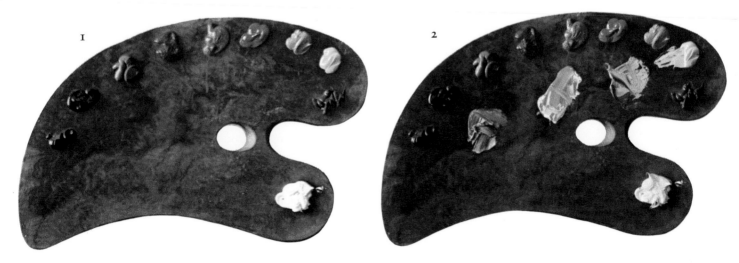

using gouache or acrylics which dry more quickly.

The principal defects of oil painting are generally failures of technique or preparation on the part of the painter. There are two main danger points to guard against: the first of these is an incorrectly prepared support surface, and the second is a careless technique when actually applying the paint. If the support is not prepared properly, the paint can lift and also suffer from attacks by dampness. If the application of the paint is incorrect, the paint film itself is liable to crack and shrivel. But do not be frightened off by these two warnings; they are given only to prevent disappointment, and in both cases, if a few very simple basic instructions are followed, can easily be avoided. If the advice on the preparation of support and technique which follows is made use of, there should be no trouble.

When making a start with oils, resist the temptation to buy a large number of different colours. Those that are recommended on page 21, are quite sufficient and until their possibilities have been fully explored should not be added to. Oil painting perhaps more than other techniques is something which must be mastered by simplified steps. A great bundle of brushes, rows of bottles containing oils, varnishes and spirits will not help; in fact they will only confuse. The number of brushes mentioned on page 23 will enable a start to be made. Oil-painting brushes are nearly always made from hog bristle because the strength and resilience of the bristles are needed to manipulate the colours satisfactorily. On your painting table or by your easel have a jar of turpentine substitute for brush cleaning. Try and develop the habit between each change of colour or mixture of thoroughly rinsing out your brushes in the turpentine substitute and then wipe through on a painting rag. At the end of a painting session the brushes, whether of hog bristle or hair, should be washed thoroughly with good plain soap or soft soap and warm water, gently scrubbing them round on the palm of the hand to remove all the colour. When they are clean they should be gently reshaped with the finger tips and then left in an upright position to dry.

The three principal supports for oils are canvas, board panels and heavy paper. The first undoubtedly is the most pleasurable to paint on and in many ways the most satisfactory. A canvas, however, is comparatively expensive and for the beginner a panel from heavy cardboard or hardboard is all right.

Ready-stretched and primed canvases can be bought from the art shops and these are normally properly prepared, but a good quality canvas should be chosen. It is noticed, regrettably, that a number of the makers of the commercially stretched canvases today use steel staples to attach the canvas to the stretchers; these staples should be replaced with copper tacks for greater permanence, as the steel staples, in a damp climate, can soon rust and rot the canvas.

Many painters prefer to prepare their canvases themselves and it certainly helps to get a greater understanding of the whole technique of oils if this is done. The material chosen can be of high quality flax linen canvas or cheaper grades of cotton canvas, sail cloth, hessian and even sacking. Man-made fibres

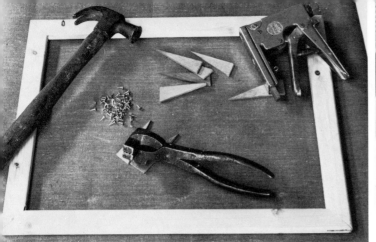

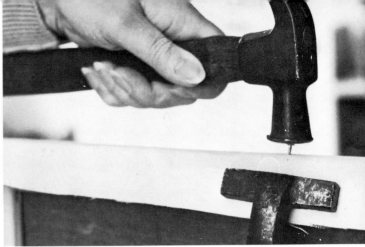

such as nylon should not be used as they are liable to lose shape and also can be affected by oil and pollutants in the air. The wooden stretchers should be stout enough for the canvas size; all too often one sees stretchers for a 25″ (625 mm) × 30″ (750 mm) picture which are only about 1½″ (40 mm) wide. Quite obviously these will not be strong enough to maintain the tension of the canvas and will be liable to warp. A 25″ (625 mm) × 30″ (750 mm) stretcher should be 2½″ (65 mm) wide at least. When selecting stretchers, pick those which fit snugly together at the corners, have a slight bevel on the front, and also have gently rounded edges to prevent chafing of the canvas.

To stretch a canvas properly, a pair of canvas straining pliers will be needed, a light hammer and a box of copper tacks. The procedure is that first a piece of canvas should be cut that will be about 3″ (75 mm) larger all the way round than the size of the stretcher. The tacking of the canvas to the stretcher is carried out to a carefully ordered pattern: first, a tack is put through the edge of the canvas in the middle of one of the sides. The stretcher and canvas are then turned over. The canvas is tightened with the aid of the straining pliers, and a tack is put in opposite to the first one. The procedure is then repeated for the other two sides. Next, working towards one corner at a time, using the straining pliers, the canvas is tacked down to the edge of the stretcher all the way round. It is important that the lines of the weave are kept at right angles to each other and parallel to the relative side of the stretcher. If this is not done, distortion of the canvas can appear at a later time. To complete the tacking, the canvas and the stretcher are laid face down and the loose edges are tacked down on to the back of the stretcher and the corners then are neatly folded over and fastened down.

Raw canvas, before painting on it with oils, has to be sized and primed. The size can be prepared either from a household decorators' packet of size, or better still from weak rabbit-skin glue. About half-an-ounce (15 g) of glue to one pint (6 dl) of water will be sufficient to isolate the canvas and prevent oil soaking into it and causing it to rot. When the coat of size has dried a priming should be prepared: this may be one of the proprietary brands sold by the colour makers; good quality household lead undercoat; or a good quality emulsion paint. One coat normally will be sufficient but a second will give a better painting surface. If the textile chosen has a very rough surface like sacking or hessian, it is a good plan to gently sandpaper away the long wispy hairs for

Steps in stretching a canvas. (1) Materials laid out. These include: wooden stretcher, canvas, copper tacks, straining pliers, wedges and stapler that can be used for small canvases provided copper staples are employed.

(2) A start is made by first putting a tack or staple through the canvas in the middle of one of the long sides of the stretcher. The canvas and stretcher are then up-ended and using the straining pliers the canvas is pulled tight and another tack or staple is driven home. The process is repeated round the various sides of the stretcher until the canvas is secure. Next it is laid face down and the edges are fixed on to the back of the stretcher and the corners are neatly tacked down.

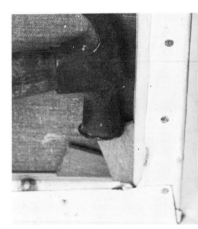

(3) Finally wedges are driven into the mitred corners of the stretcher to give further tightening if needed.

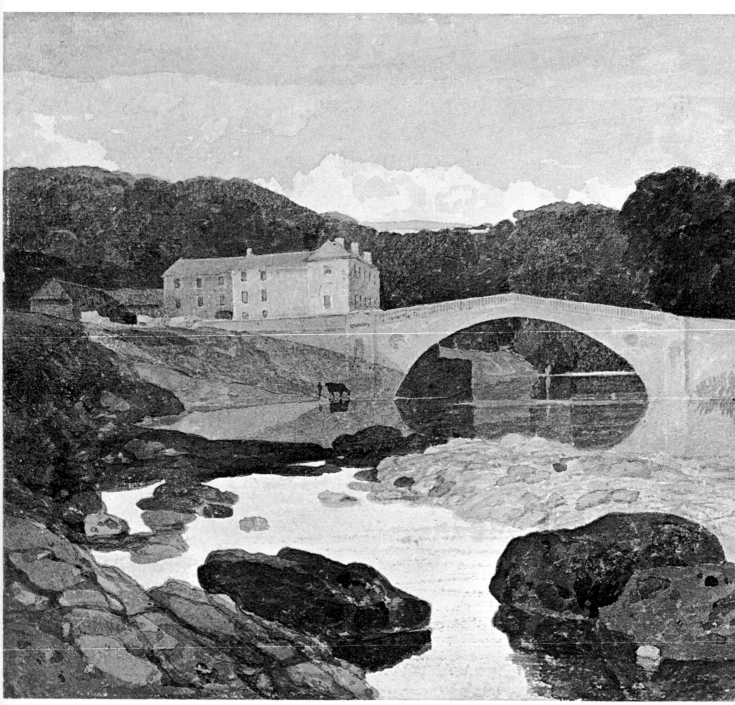

John Sell Cotman: Greta Bridge
(Watercolour and gouache)
British Museum, London (page 47)

An exquisitely balanced
composition with the severe
symmetry of the bridge being
broken by the buildings to
the left and the trees to the
right. A subject such as
this which has extreme dark
next to light areas could be
partially handled by using
masking fluid.

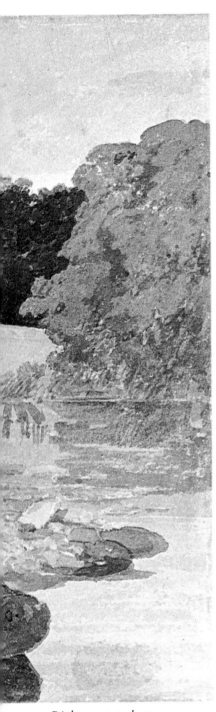

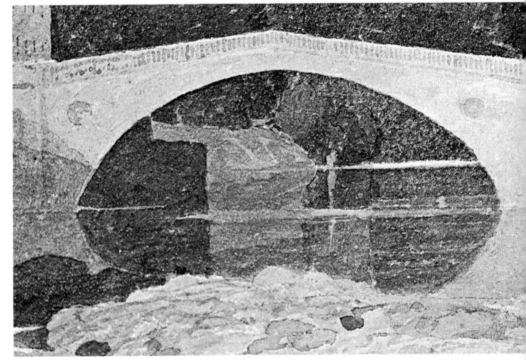

Right – top to bottom
The details show the
treatment of: the white
clouds in the centre
distance: the bridge and
reflections: the large boulders
in the foreground.

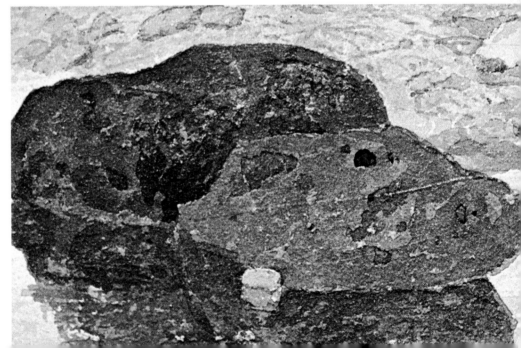

if left they will only cause trouble. The priming can be given a rougher surface if a little whiting or coarse marble dust is added to it, but certainly this proportion should not exceed one part additive to ten parts of priming.

If a card, hardboard or wooden panel is chosen to paint on, it should always be battened if its size makes it liable to warp. Card, hardboard and wood should all be sized and primed as is the case with canvas. If a really smooth surface is wanted, an application of gesso can be made to hardboard and wood as described on page 38. Gesso should not be put on cardboard, as the material is too weak and is liable to bend or move and so crack the gesso. A number of painters prefer to use thick paper for oil sketches, and the only treatment this needs is a coat of size to prevent the paper soaking up the oil from the paint and so weakening its adherence.

Mediums

Oil paints are prepared by the pigments being ground, generally, in linseed oil, and as they are finished and packed in the tubes the colours often do not need much in the way of liquid mediums to be added to them for normal painting. It is wise when buying the colours to open one or two tubes and inspect the condition of the paints. If there are drops of free oil, it probably means that the milling has been incorrectly done, and in any case the colours will be too slack. A gentle squeeze will soon show if the paint has the correct degree of stiffness or is 'short' so that it will faithfully hold the texture of brush and knife strokes. Good quality oil paint should be able to stand up straight at least half-an-inch (15 mm) from the neck of the tube.

If the paint needs to be diluted, the choice lies between the use of more linseed oil, poppy oil, nut oil, turpentine, turpentine substitute, or one or other of the makers' proprietary mediums. Only experience can really make the decision. More linseed oil will increase the flow of the colour and to a certain extent it will also increase the time of drying. Poppy oil will still further increase the time of drying and is often used by portrait painters when they want to work over an area for an appreciable time. Turpentine and turpentine substitute will shorten the time of drying and can be used for quick oil sketches, or are very suitable for putting in the layers of underpainting. The characteristics of the makers' mediums will generally be stated on the bottles. Some of these mediums may be mixtures of oils and varnishes which can give added richness to some colours. On the whole, avoid mixing drying oils or drying agents with your colours as these can cause trouble between layers, and also cracking.

Varnishes

An oil painting needs to be varnished for two reasons. The first is that the varnish helps to restore the brilliant visual effect of the original wet paint, an effect which tends to tone down after a week or two. The second is that varnish provides a protection for the paint from the atmosphere. It is really better never to put an oil painting behind glass as, although this may give it surface protection, it makes it more difficult to see, and in damp climates can encourage mould growths.

Before about 1950 practically all oil paintings were varnished with copal, dammar or mastic varnish. These are all natural resins and to a lesser or greater degree all have the same defects: they are liable to become brittle and crack; in damp atmospheres they can bloom and with time gradually go darker and darker yellow. The modern water-clear synthetic resin varnishes have by now been tested sufficiently to show that they are a safe substitute. The tricky decision to make is whether it is better to use a gloss varnish, or a mat varnish which has probably had some wax added to it or some matting agent. Aesthetically most people today would plum for the mat surface, as this does allow the picture to be seen clearly from any angle. The possible exception to this is where the painting has large areas of dark umbers, blacks, or crimsons for often a glossy varnish will bring these out better than a mat, and if the picture is hung with a cross light it can be viewed perfectly.

An oil painting, particularly if there are areas of heavy impasto, should not be varnished for at least twelve months after the painting is finished. It will take all of this time for the paint to harden out sufficiently. Whenever convenient, varnishing should be done on a dry day and in as dust-free an atmosphere as possible. The picture should be laid flat on a table and the varnish applied quickly with a wide, flat white hog-bristle varnish brush. It should be applied with short criss-cross strokes, with as even a film as can be achieved. Modern synthetic varnishes often dry in under the hour.

There is one other type of varnish which is useful to have; this is known as retouching varnish. Its purpose is twofold. First, it can be brushed over an area that has gone flat during the painting, this will help restore the visual effect. Secondly, it can be used as a temporary varnish for a picture which is already skin-dry. This would be useful if there was a special exhibition coming up or it was necessary to show the painting to a client. Retouching varnish is very thin and therefore the drying process exerts little tension on the paint layers beneath and will not cause them to crack.

Palettes

The choice of a palette for oil painting is, again, something that will need personal experience. If you are going to work outside, the palette should be one that can be held in the hand and may be either mahogany or one of the disposable paper varieties. The latter have their uses as they save much time at the end of the day; all that needs to be done is for the sheet of greaseproof paper with the paint to be pulled away from the pack and disposed of. Mahogany

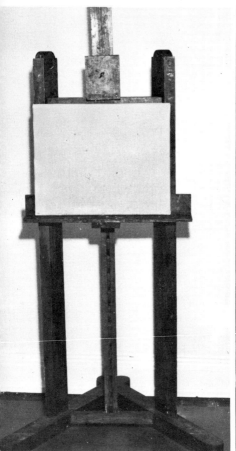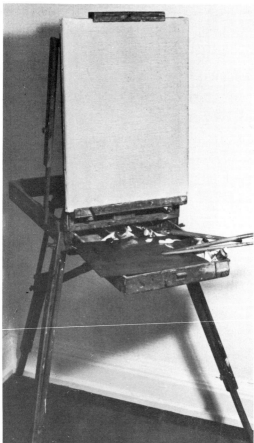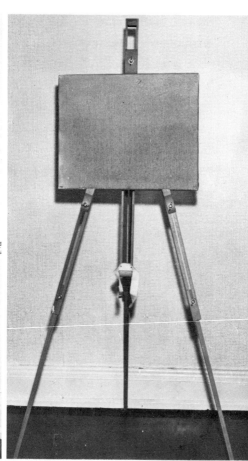

Left. Hardwood studio easel. The height is controlled by a catch and ratchet. Canvases up to about forty by fifty inches (101 × 127 cm) can be used and are held in place with a wing-screw secured guillotine head.

Centre. Box sketching easel. One of the most convenient for out-door work. The drawer holds paints, brushes and knives, and a rectangular palette fixes in place as a lid. It will take a canvas up to about twenty-eight by thirty-six inches (71 × 91 cm) which can be carried clipped into the easel.

Right. The simplest form of sketching easel. Only really suitable for a canvas up to about twenty-five by thirty inches (63 × 76 cm). Greater stability can be obtained by suspending a stone on a string from the bolt securing the three legs.

palettes today always seem to be a little 'hungry'. Before use they should be given a little soaking with linseed oil and left for a few days. The excess oil can then be wiped away and after about a further seven days the palette will be ready for use. If this treatment is given, it will greatly improve the surface of the palette for mixing colours on. Working in the studio, recourse can be made to a large sheet of plate glass, as mentioned for acrylics on page 40. If oil colour hardens out on a wooden or a glass palette, the quickest treatment is to scrape off what you can and then soak the remainder with a non-caustic commercial paint remover. Leave for about five minutes, scrape off the remainder and wipe clean with a piece of rag and turpentine substitute.

Easels

One piece of equipment can perhaps be avoided with acrylics and watercolour, but for oil painting it is a must; this item is an easel. In many ways the main consideration will be cost. A light sketching easel can be bought fairly cheaply, but a full-size studio easel with gears that will raise and lower the canvas and give it a tilt can cost from up to £200 or more. There are two principal factors, steadiness and an ability to hold the canvas firm. If you are intending to paint mostly out-of-doors, some form of light-weight easel that will fold up – and which has not too many complicated joints to be worked out when erecting it –

will be essential. One of the better types, which is well worth a few pounds, is a box easel which will carry the brushes and tubes and generally has a palette that is used as a lid. This type of easel will hold a canvas up to 28″ (700 mm) × 36″ (910 mm) quite happily, and many of them are so designed that when collapsed for carrying, the wet canvas can be clamped into position and receive some protection for that generally awkward journey home.

If working in a studio, an easel of a somewhat heavier construction is better, as the greater weight of timber will add to stability. There is a type that stands on three well-splayed legs that will provide a tilt and hold a canvas up to six feet high. There are also a number of tubular metal easels which may be all right when they are new but tend to become bent and dented with use.

Preliminary technique

Many painters like to use an 'imprimatura'. This is a toned layer on top of the priming. The purpose of an imprimatura is to kill the frightening white of the canvas and also to help the picture come together in its initial stages. A number of great artists have used toned canvases. Holbein sometimes liked a diluted dark blue; Rubens used pale green; and Constable preferred a red ochre. It can be noted in some of Constable's pictures how areas of the imprimatura have been left showing through in the shadows and dark areas as part of the colour scheme. The imprimatura should be put over the priming as a thin wash and given at least twenty-four hours to dry out before painting begins.

The principal rule to remember in painting with oils is to follow the house-painter's theory of 'start lean, finish fat'. This means that underpainting should be carried out using turpentine or turpentine substitute to thin down the paint and so reduce its richness and at the same time increase its speed of drying. Much of the trouble with cracking and rivelling with oil paintings is caused by the breaking of this simple rule. If the early layers of a painting are put on too thick and rich and then later layers are applied before the first are completely hard, an argument is set up between the two films drying out, one against the other, at different speeds. The result is that something has to give.

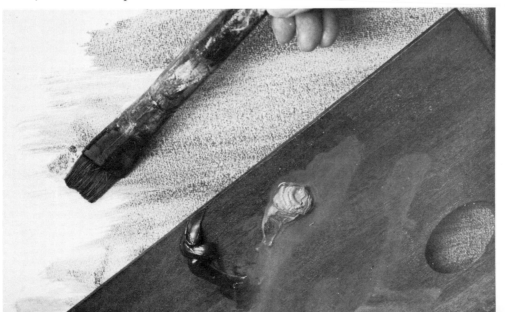

Laying an 'imprimatura'. It is often desirable to work from a toned ground. This may be of a colour to suit the individual case. Burnt Umber, Burnt Sienna or Raw Umber are favourites. The colour should be applied well diluted with turpentine substitute. It should not be put on mixed with oil as this could lay a rich fatty coat that would take a long time to dry and which could encourage cracking when the painting itself is completed. Here a mixture of Burnt Umber and Yellow Ochre is being used.

There are many theories about the best method of preliminary drawing-in for an oil painting; charcoal and pencil are advocated, but both of these have the drawback that the black from the charcoal and the graphite from the pencil are liable to adulterate the colours when they are applied. By far the best way is to use the same method as for acrylics or watercolour. With a fairly small round brush mix up to a liquid wash consistency some burnt umber, French ultramarine and turpentine substitute, and use this for the simple drawing-in. If a mistake is made, it can be easily eradicated by wiping off with a paint rag dipped in turpentine substitute. Deliberately keep the drawing-in as simple as possible. View your subject and analyse it as to the main masses and striking points; these are all that should be indicated at the initial stage. If you concentrate too much on the intricacies of detail, you will do two things: first, you will constrict the progress of the picture, as you may feel you should follow through accurately each of these small details; secondly, you will defeat the main purpose of oil painting in its most general sense, and that is, the suggestion only of detail. The building up of the facets of the subject is done by brush-strokes, painting knives, and textures.

Underpainting, if desired, may be done either as a monochrome or as an understatement of the final colours. If it is done as a monochrome, this could be kept to tones related to the imprimatura and just the main masses of light and shade and principal modelling indicated. Where the underpainting is in colour it opens wide fields for experiment. The chief reason Rubens used a green underpainting for his flesh was that he was using the complementary theory of colours opposite one another in the colour circle supporting each other; for example, crimson underpainting for heavy textured grass on a field. But whatever variation of this is experimented with, follow the rule that all the underpainting must be thin and lean. It is safe practice to underpaint for oils with egg tempera, and this has been done by many artists. The egg tempera should be kept thin and allowed to dry for at least forty-eight hours before painting over it.

At the start, a little practice is desirable to familarize oneself with the mixing characteristics of oil colours. When setting the colours out on the palette, keep them well to the edge to leave as much space as possible free for mixing. Get into the habit of putting the colours down in the same order, as this will be a time-saver during painting. A good method is to have the dark colours, like burnt umber, to the left and the bright red and yellows to the right, beside a large lump of white. In painting with oils, white is used to a large extent rather like water with watercolour; it is used to dilute or 'break' the other colours to obtain lighter tones.

Always draw colour away from the main piles on the palette, using a clean brush; if this is not done, much paint will be wasted by pollution. Experiment with one colour after another, mixing in different amounts of white. It is often surprising how some colours appear to change character when they are mixed with large quantities of white. Try out mixes between the various colours at full strength and also when they are mixed with white. It will be found that the comparatively short list of colours suggested can provide an almost infinite variety of tints and tones. Dark pungent greens can come from yellow and black; soft warm greys from red, blue, yellow and white. The more time that can be spent on this preliminary exercise the better, as at each stroke of the brush knowledge and understanding will be picked up for use when the actual painting begins.

Alla prima

This term means literally completing an oil painting in one sitting. If working in this manner there is no worry as to various layers of colour fighting one against the other as the whole will be done in one application. Alla prima painting for many has a great attraction, because it can capture a sense of freshness and excitement. But, as with watercolour, it does need careful planning and an absolutely direct and sure approach. If a mistake is made, it can of course be scraped away with a knife and wiped clean with a rag, but it is very difficult to disguise; it is rather as though an accident had happened to a piece of tapestry, some of the threads had been torn away and then they had to be exactly matched. In some ways an alla prima painting has a relationship with tapestry or embroidery, in that the whole is made up of countless brush-strokes of different colours which interweave with each other; thus, as far as possible, each of those strokes must be put down correctly the first time.

Painting with oils, particularly in this manner, is different from other media. The artist should stand up, preparations made, in front of his easel, eye his subject, concentrate on the canvas and mentally sense the whole build-up before making the actual physical contact with the brush. Probably more time will be taken looking and thinking than with the actual painting. But, if this method is adopted, it is much more likely to produce success. If painting directly in an alla prima manner, it is near fatal to the result to just keep on paddling away at the canvas without *seeing* the result of each stroke before making it. All too often beginners make a mad rush at their canvas or panel; perhaps this is a form of nerves; but the result is that they almost inevitably make a bad start, become frustrated and, worse, can lose heart.

A brush-stroke in oil painting is a much more sensitive thing than with water-colour. Oil colours, if correctly formulated, are designed so that they will hold the exact mark of the brush. This is the painter's handwriting and is one of the principal ways a picture can be recognised as by a known master. It is also one of the tricks which the forger struggles hardest to copy. Examine paintings by Frans Hals, Rubens, Raeburn, Seurat, Van Gogh, and Francis Bacon: artists of different periods, and each of them with highly distinctive handwriting in their paint. Observe also pictures by these men and others and note the ever-changing variety of stroke and texture over the whole picture area. Nothing is more damning to the vitality of a painting than monotony of brush-work; as for example, if a broad expanse of blue sky is simply indicated by repetitive horizontal strokes. In this context, a study of the French Impressionists, the works of Monet, Pissarro and Sisley, can be most illuminating. What was the magic that gave their paintings the feeling of real atmosphere? Close to, the answer is evident; superb brush-work and the use of 'broken colour'. They realized that there are very few instances of completely flat colour in nature. Reflected lights, reflected colours, shadows, half-shadows, all play their part in building up variety.

Try to visualize the composition of the different objects and areas of the subject and analyse these so that they may be simulated with brush-strokes. The different shapes of brush, as was discussed on page 23 all have the means of making their own individual marks. The painter seeks to exploit these. Imagination is needed not only in seeing a picture but also in the use of the available materials.

In the laying-on of the thick oil colours in direct painting there need not be a feeling of limitation, as for instance that two wet strokes must not touch in case they bleed or mix together. This will only happen if the brush is applied with an unsure feeling or the colour is puddled around on the canvas. The secret here is to swallow your fear, take that long understanding look, pick up the paint from the palette with the brush and place it precisely and crisply on to the canvas. If this is done, it is quite possible to put wet against wet and even to take a wet stroke across an already laid wet area without bleeding or spoiling.

One serious error, which is all too often seen with beginners, is the using of the canvas as the palette. The colours put on appear to be wrong and an attempt is made to rectify them by mixing and rubbing together on the canvas. This is nearly always a disaster and as a general rule should not be done. All colour mixing should be carried out on the palette and more than that it should be done as directly as possible. Try to make your mix between two or more colours on the palette with as few strokes as you can; in this way the finally applied colours will 'sing' out, but if they are continuously stirred on the palette with a brush or a knife, they very soon come down to a flat and rather sordid mud. Muddy colours are the hallmark of indecision and lack of thought before painting.

When using a knife with oils it is even more important to make certain of a direct approach, as colours put on with broad sweeping strokes by a painting knife can have subtleties of tint and tone which are impossible to re-achieve if a correction has to be made. Note some of the exquisite colour effects by Vlaminck. In his skies and foregrounds there are often large areas of beautifully modulated colour put in by sweeping strokes that are the epitome of the alla prima approach.

Underpainting and overpainting

On a previous page we discussed the laying-in of preliminary undercoats which might be monochrome or coloured. These early coats act as the foundation for the final painting. For many painters this method has a distinct attraction because it allows more definite planning and a consistent build-up of the areas of the picture. Provided the underpainting is lean and has dried out, the method is just as safe from the permanent point of view as alla prima. It is important, however, when overpainting is carried out with oils to understand that the medium, although primarily opaque, does have one pecularity; so called *pentimenti* can appear several years afterwards. Pentimenti are produced when light colours are laid over dark colours or preliminary drawings which have been altered and not erased. Gradually with time a ghosting through appears, which can be very unsightly and throw out the whole composition. Therefore if a change is felt necessary between the final painting and the underpainting it is safest to make the correction in the underlayers before proceeding.

When a painter comes to complete a picture which has been underpainted, he is much freer to concentrate on his textures and colours because all the main decisions of light, shade and modelling have already been made with the underpainting. He can now develop the whole picture from this foundation. The imprimatura and the underpainting mean that there is no staring white to cover and the way is clear to use all the imagination, as well as the results of experiments, to achieve one's own individual manner.

The colour can be put on in many ways at this stage. There can be the direct straightforward stroke attack. There can be scumbling of one colour over another; the attraction of this is that a broken effect can be attained, the idea being that the colour is dragged or pushed across another earlier dry one, so that part of the first shows through; this can be done with a flat brush held almost parallel to the canvas or with a finger tip or a knuckle.

Broken colour can be put on with a continuous brush-stroke by using the following device. Select a round brush and then very carefully load it at one point with a colour, turn it slightly and pick up another related colour, and turn again and pick up a third and even a fourth colour. The colours chosen could, for example, be light cadmium yellow, deep cadmium yellow, yellow ochre, and a mixture of yellow ochre and burnt umber. The brush is then taken to the canvas and the stroke applied with the brush being revolved as it is pulled down, the result: a series of broken colours which could simulate a freshly driven sawn post.

Telegraph lines, electric power cables, or riggings of ships sometimes pose problems. They can, of course, be put in using a long-haired rigger, with the colour diluted with oil, and the hand steadied by a mahlstick held in the other hand. But with a free expressive manner of painting this could appear laborious. A more successful method is to select a piece of thin string or thread and along

The use of a Mahlstick to
steady the hand when
working on a detail with a
'rigger'.

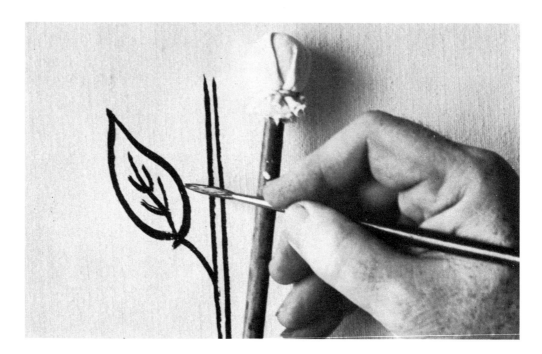

its length pick up the chosen colour and then manoeuvre it so that it just
touches the right area of the canvas and leaves its mark.

Generally speaking, it is wise not to try putting additives such as kaolin,
marble dust or whiting into oil colours. It may stiffen the paint but it is almost
certain to affect the permanence, and the colour so treated is liable to crack and
flake in the future.

Glazing

This is one of the most exciting and least used methods with oils. If properly
handled it can bring out almost a new dimension. The principle is that transparent or near-transparent colours are diluted with an oil and are then glazed
or overlaid on previously dried out colours. The effect achieved can be rich,
translucent, and evocative of the jewel-like appearance of stained glass.
Obviously glazing needs very careful planning and a complete understanding of
the reaction of one colour seen through the transparency of another. Here
again, experiments on odd pieces of canvas or hardboard are essential so that
the possibilities can be sensed. The application of the glazes is a matter of
choice, but probably they are more easily applied using a large soft-haired
brush and with the canvas or the panel at an angle of about fifteen degrees
rather than vertical. If a mistake is made it should be possible with care to
remove this with a piece of clean rag and turpentine substitute. Obviously
allow time for the surface to dry before another attempt is made.

A second approach to glazing is to use a monochrome underpainting. This
should be carried out in fairly pale tones of warm grey, so that all the actual
colour will be obtained by the transparent glazes. Properly handled this can
give great subtlety and quality to the result. Pictures may also be carried out by

glazed techniques alone applied to a white ground using the stark qualities of the white to light up the individual colours.

Freedom

As experience is gained so will fears and restrictive feelings drop away. The success will be judged not so much by the way the picture has been painted as by the result that hangs on the wall. If the way to that result has been laboured and filled with sorrow these will show. The paint will lack sparkle, the whole will probably be drab and dull of tone. If there has been enjoyment and attack these will show just as surely on the canvas.

It has been underlined earlier that a few basic rules must be watched with oils. These need not be limiting. Once they have been observed they can be liberating, as from then on more experiments can be tried and new ground ventured upon. It is with the actual putting on of the paint that personal imagination can be let loose.

Besides brushes and knives the colours can be manipulated with forms of sgraffito, using the pointed ends of brushes and small pieces of wood to cut through and expose the imprimatura or white priming. The fingers and thumbs have been used by painters for centuries. Each new way will leave a distinctive mark in the paint which will add to the textures, the paint film and the general sense of life.

Professor Tonks, the famous teacher at the Slade, employed an off-beat manner when, after he had put on his paint, he spread a sheet of clean paper over the surface, gently smoothed it down with his hand and then, raising one end, peeled it away so that it lifted off much of the colour. The effect of this is to produce an overall softening which can be very attractive. Sometimes if a painting as it is proceeded with becomes overladen with paint and out of control it can be rescued by 'tonking'. Incidentally often it can be found that the sheet of paper lifted off with the excess colour is itself an interesting monotype.

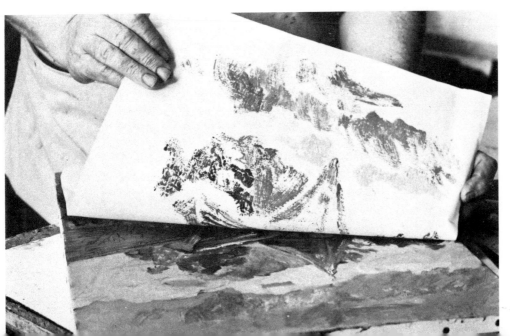

Sometimes overworked areas of a painting become almost clogged with too much colour. It is possible to remove this and still retain the shape of the composition. The process known as 'Tonking' consists of laying a clean sheet of paper across the picture and then gently smoothing it down with the palm of the hand. It can then be lifted clear with the excess paint.

The mechanics

Although it has been stressed that freedom in painting is important, there are some guide-lines that can make the effort simpler. Even with the broadest 'way-out' abstract or piece of tachism there is always some skeleton of construction, some thesis on which it is built. Examples are often shown of how the 'Old Masters' worked to carefully triangulated systems of pictorial arrangement. Whether this was their intention or whether it was that they had a natural sense of balance and placing, so perfect that it allowed for a geometric translation, is a point for discussion.

The building up of the main masses in a picture, no matter what the subject, must be correct or, however well painted, the final result will be unsatisfactory. This composing of the picture is something that calls for rather more than just physical means – for a sensitive mental appraisal of the process as it is put down. A picture with good composition is one that appears absolutely at ease within the borders of the frame. No matter whether the subject is a bowl of flowers, a calm scene at sea or an action-packed battle, the same simple basic rules lie beneath it. Composition, to be successful, implies the imposition of an harmonious arrangement of not only shapes and lines but also colour, shade and high-lit areas.

There are a few basic errors that are liable to crop up and need watching out for. If painting a landscape, it is unwise to divide the picture exactly in two by the horizon line; the result will generally be monotonous. It is better to have the dividing line between sky and land either above or below the centre, depending on where the viewpoint is. In the same manner any subject, whether landscape, still life or interior should not be divided exactly in two vertically.

The proportion of the main masses one to another and in particular to the canvas area needs care. If a flower arrangement is being painted it should sit quite happily into the rectangle. It does not want to be too far either to one side or the other or to the top or the bottom; nor does it want to be overdrawn so that some features actually are cut by the mount or the frame. Any of these points are liable to give the impression that the painting has been cut down from its original intended size. Again, beware of under-drawing so that the main subject stands tiny and lonely in the middle of large expanses of canvas.

Under the heading of arrangement can come the two opposite terms of

Opposite:

Still life composition. *Top.*
(1) In setting up a still life the objects should rest harmoniously within the rectangle of the canvas or panel. Try to pick subjects that will contrast in texture. Note here the shells, the brass and the glass in the lamp; the rough earthenware in the pot at the back, the hard glaze on the tea-pot, and the soft underlying material.

(2) Watch that the main group is not placed too far to one side, as this can give the impression that the painting has been cut down. Likewise the same effect could happen if the group were too far to the top or the bottom.

Below. (3) Don't be timid and have the group too small, lost in the middle of the canvas.

(4) In contrast to the foregoing, it is almost worse to have the group too large and bursting out of the borders of the picture.

symmetry and asymmetry. Sometimes in choosing a subject it is possible to be confronted with a piece of perfect symmetry, whether in a landscape or with flowers or an interior. Broadly speaking, it is often wiser to break the symmetry, so that the composition is asymmetrical, and will be more interesting to the eye. However, at this point, there always seems to be the master hand which mocks the suggested rule. An outstanding example of a symmetrical masterpiece is the *Avenue Middelharnis* by Hobbema in the National Gallery, London. Perhaps it is that real talent, once it has digested all the rules and methods, arrives at a complete freedom which finds laws for success from itself.

The main intention of composition is to produce a balance, a harmony, an interest; all three of which join to extend an invitation to the viewer's eye to enter the picture and explore. This invitation can be further strengthened by the use of light and shade, colour control and perspective.

Without light, nothing, quite obviously, would have any meaning, form or

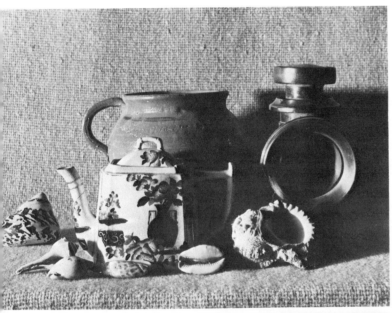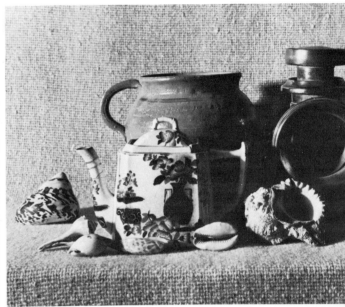

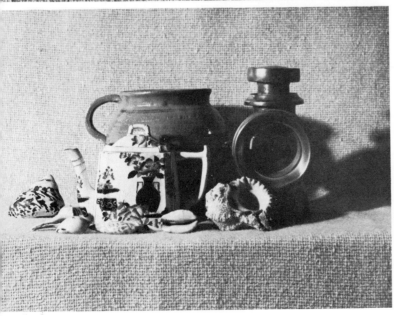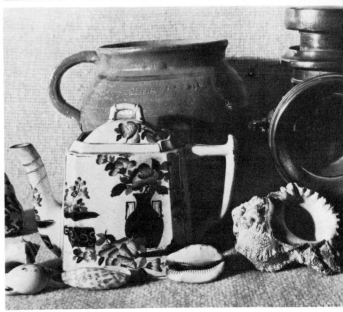

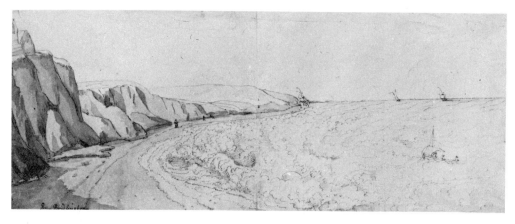

colour. Light to the painter is the most vital factor: without it there is no sub-stance. Light and its product, shade, produce areas which from the composition point of view are as solid as rocks, trees and buildings. The direction and control of the light needs observation and if necessary calculated arrangement. If the same scene is painted at eight o'clock in the morning, at midday and at six in the evening, three different pictures will result. Experiment here with light coming from the left, overhead and the right. The first and last will probably produce the most interesting results, whilst the example with the light directly overhead will tend to look unnatural and a little empty as very few large areas of shadow will be produced, other than deep patches underneath the trees or from large overhangs on buildings.

The varying intensities of light run through a whole range of subtleties: the gentle reflected light that creeps from behind a round form on the side away from the highlight; the bright splashes of full sunlight that fall on a path, filtered by the leafy tree-tops; the sharp sparkle of the highlight on a glass or glazed pottery vessel; the rays of light that pour from behind a cloud; the dusty beams that lance through a crack in a door or shutter. With the light comes its partner, shadow. In between there are the half-tones and numerous soft, almost indistinguishable nuances. Observe, note and experiment with the handling of light and shade in all their various moods. The colour in shadows calls for the acutest vision; in the interplay of tones and tints there is so much variety – never dull dark grey or near-black flat areas.

Too many suggestions for colour handling in painting can stultify ambition.

Below. Lighting. *Left*. The light source is one of the most important features in picture-making. This illustration and the two that follow it show how a variation in the light direction to a degree makes a different picture each time. Here the light is from the left.

Centre. Here the light is coming from directly overhead.

Right. Lastly, with the light from the right.

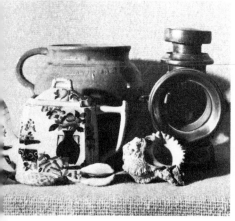
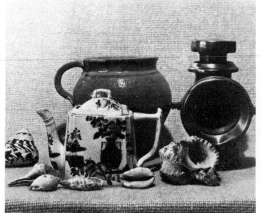
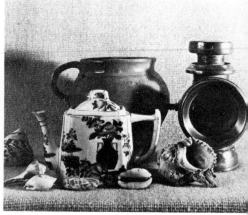

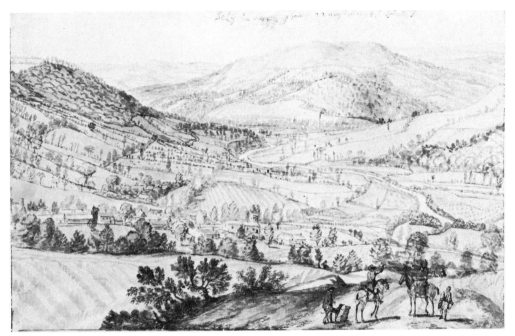

Jan Siberechts: Beeley, near Chatsworth
(watercolours and body colours with white)
A high horizon is almost obligatory when depicting ranges of mid-distant and distant high hills.
British Museum, London

Too much dabbling with complicated theories can bog down the attack. In general, watch the tonal strengths and tints of colours: the nearer the foreground the stronger and warmer; as they recede, lighter and cooler. The lighter tones and colours are often more difficult to judge than the darker. The sky can be deceptive on a clear day; it gives the immediate appearance of coming down blue right to the horizon – but there is so much dust in the atmosphere that the bottom of the sky above the horizon will tend towards pinky, warm grey. Shiny surfaces, as with painted doors or polished metal, will tend to show colour reflected from objects nearest to them.

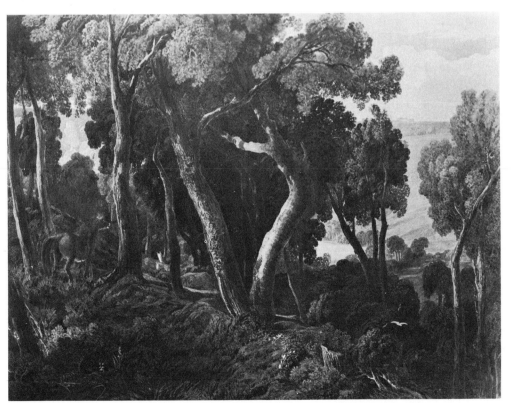

William Turner of Oxford: Wychwood Forest, Oxfordshire
(watercolour)
Note the right-hand tree in the centre. Maximum feeling of roundness is completed by the observation of reflected light. This has been put in on the opposite side to the highlight.
Victoria and Albert Museum, London

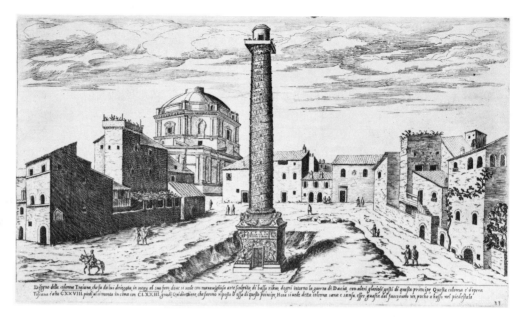

Etienne du Perac: The Trajan Column
(engraving)
The central placing of the column and the arrangement of the buildings produce a near symmetrical effect and thus the eye is not really invited to explore the composition. More than this, the central placing of the strong vertical feature cuts the composition in half.
Victoria and Albert Museum, London

The complementary colour theory is worth trying, to obtain a particular accent or where a 'lift' is called for. Briefly, it means, that colours on opposite sides of a primary and secondary colour circle will react best together. Thus, red against green, yellow against purple, blue set beside orange. Variations of these will allow for infinite experiment.

The early paintings of scenes with buildings often had a very strange look. This was because the artists knew nothing of how to produce a third dimensional effect. The science of perspective had not been worked out. There are geometric rules for the accurate drawing of perspectives, but these are not necessary for painting, they are more for the architect and engineer. The full rules involve plans, height lines, viewpoints, projections and more. To achieve some sense of 'third dimension', all that is needed are a few simple instructions. The simplest perspective is what is termed 'single point'. With this an horizon line is taken right across the picture area, and somewhere near the middle a

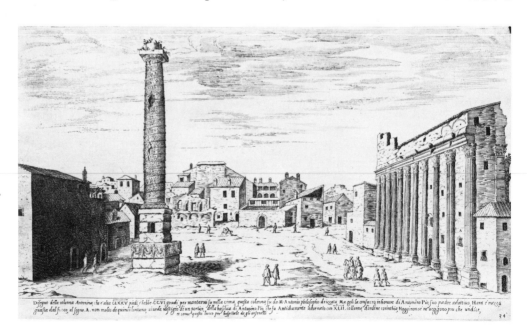

Etienne du Perac: The Antonine Column
(engraving)
Here the artist has placed a similar column to that in the illustration for symmetry, but this time to the left-hand side, and by so doing has made a more interesting composition.
Victoria and Albert Museum, London

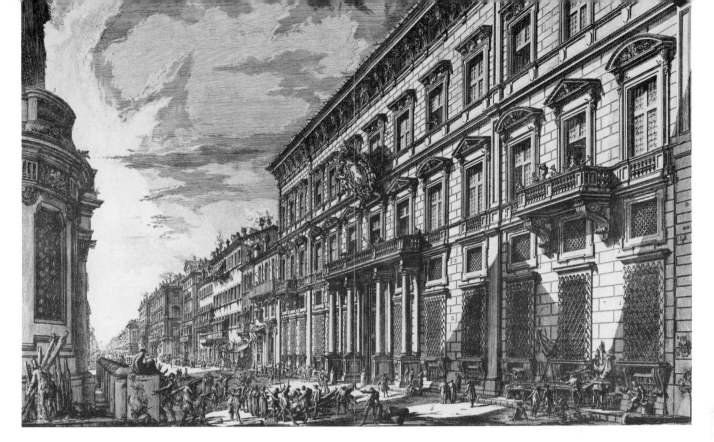

vanishing point is placed. To this vanishing point the relevant vertical and horizontal planes of the picture are aligned. This will give the characteristic vanishing effect of lines of poles or fences, of walls, as well as the impression that the sides of a road going away from the viewer will eventually meet.

A greater sense of realism can be achieved by using 'two-point' perspective. Here again an horizon line is used, and on it, at places outside the picture area, are placed two vanishing points, one on each side. It is to these two vanishing

Above. **Piranesi: Palazzo dell'accademia**
(etching)
The single vanishing point used here dramatizes the presentation of the buildings.

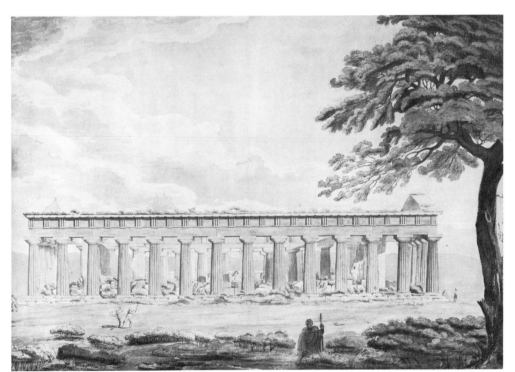

Left. **Willey Peverley: Paestum, Temple of Neptune**
(watercolour)
The dramatic presentation clearly shows the use of two vanishing points: the basis of most external perspective work.
Victoria and Albert Museum, London

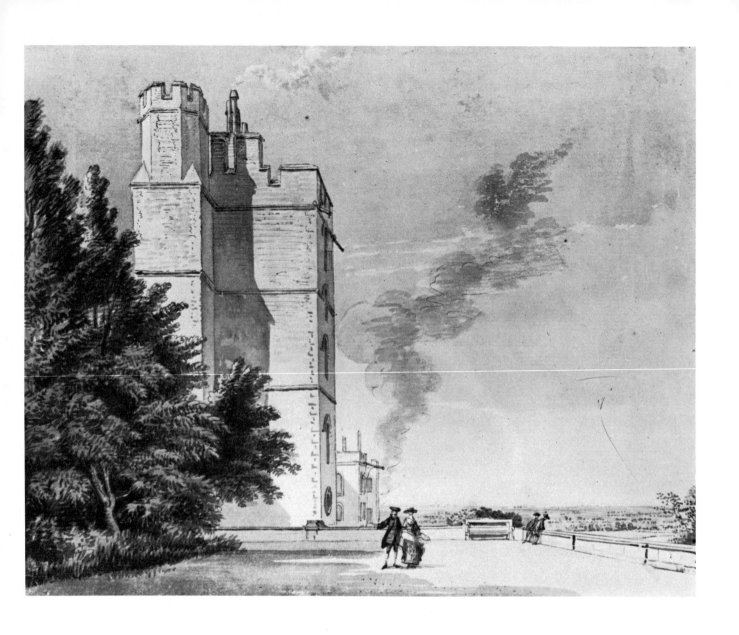

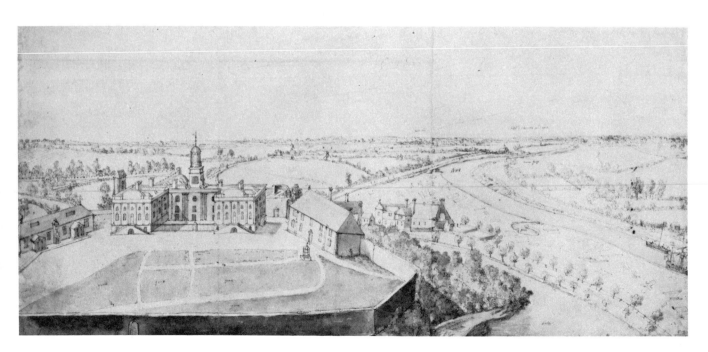

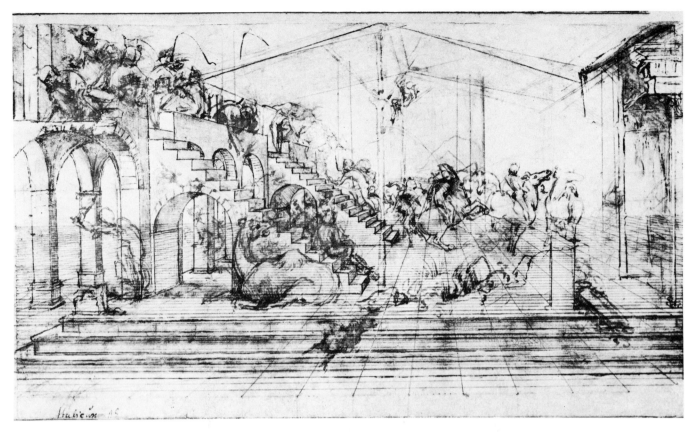

points that the relevant planes are then aligned. In both single and two-point perspective the final effect of the picture can be drastically altered by changing the position of the vanishing points. A few minutes rough sketching on a piece of paper will soon illustrate the possibilities.

If the scene is being viewed from a hill or tall building, to produce the sense of looking down on the view, what is termed 'bird's eye' perspective can be used to create the illusion. To do this, all that is required is to raise the horizon line and the vanishing points to the top of the picture area and then work as before. The opposite to 'bird's eye' is 'worm's eye', which will give the feeling of looking up at a building. Here all that is done is to lower the horizon line and the vanishing points right to the bottom of the picture. If dealing with an interior, variations of all the foregoing four methods can be employed, horizon lines and vanishing points being placed to suit the particular viewpoint.

Above. **Leonardo da Vinci: Study of the Perspective of the Background of the Adoration of the Magi** (pen and ink over metal point with some wash) In this drawing it can be noted how there is an almost centrally placed vanishing point. This can, of course, be moved to achieve various aspects. *Uffizi, Florence*

Opposite:

Top. **Paul Sandby: The North Terrace, The West End – Windsor** (pen and watercolour, traces of pencil) The low viewpoint tends to dramatize tall features and gives the impression of unusual scale. Vanishing points come down to ground level or close to it. *The Royal Library, Windsor Castle*

Opposite:

Bottom. **Francis Place: York from Cliffords Tower** (pen and brown ink, brown wash tinted in watercolour) By raising the vanishing points the impression of looking down is gained. *British Museum, London*

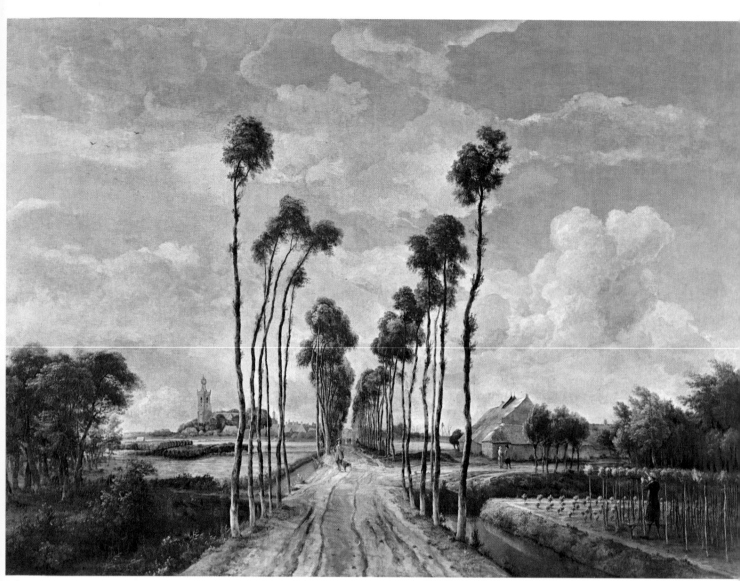

Hobbema: The Avenue, Middelharnis (1689) 1035 × 1410 mm
The National Gallery, London (pages 108/9)

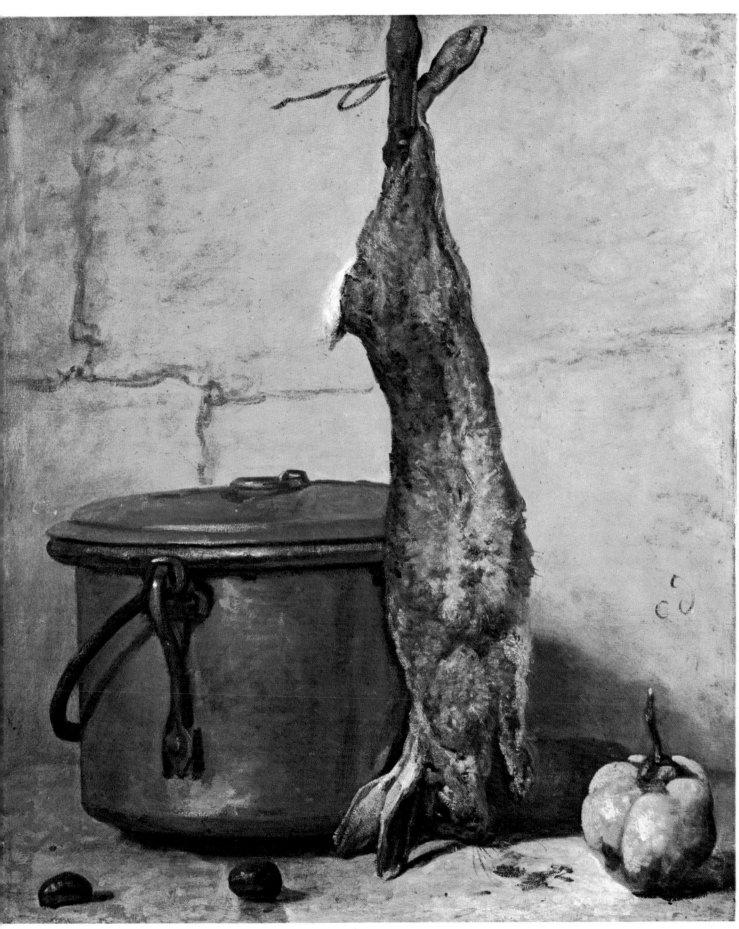

Chardin: Still Life, Hare and Copper Cauldron 680 × 570 mm
The National Museum, Stockholm (page 88)

The subject

Still life

Whatever personal prejudice may be, the wisest choice for the first subject in painting is a still life. The reason for this is that the objects can be carefully arranged, the light controlled, and you will not be concerned with movement or alteration in colour and shadows. The entire concentration can be given to painting.

The study of dead or inanimate objects by the artist goes back a long way. On a painted wooden coffin found at Al Barshah in Egypt and dating from 2400 BC are paintings of birds, fruit and utensils. This early Egyptian painter was probably thinking more about these items as symbols indicative of after-life sustenance for the departed than a composition with an aesthetic intention.

Pliny informs us that Apollodorus of Athens (*circa* 408 BC) 'was the first to paint objects as they really appeared.' Our knowledge of Greco-Roman and Roman art enables us to see that the art of many of the ancients had reached a stage close to that of sixteenth and seventeenth century European painters. Pliny in another place says: 'We must now, however, make some mention of those artists who acquired fame by the pencil in an inferior style of painting. Among these was Piraeicus, inferior to few of the painters in skill. I am not sure that he did not do injustice to himself by the choice of his subjects. . . . His subjects were barbers' shops, cobblers' stalls, jackasses, eatables, and the like, and to these he was indebted for the epithet of "Rhyparographos." His paintings, however, are exquisitely pleasing, and have sold at higher prices than the very largest works of many masters.'

Recent discoveries show that the ancients of the Hellenistic period practised and enjoyed still life very much in the same sense as the patrons and artists of the seventeenth century. There were the same kinds of subjects: dead fish, dead birds, baskets, etc. These were generally painted directly on to the walls or executed in mosaic, such as the famous pigeons on a bowl – copied from a design of Sosos of Pergamon, who is also claimed to have produced the extraordinary 'Oikos asaretos' or 'unswept floor'. This strange mosaic floor showed dining-table refuse such as might have fallen down after a banquet: chicken bones, snail shells, small cakes, fruit and vegetables.

The history of European painting which really begins with the Italian Renaissance shows many painters including still life objects in their pictures, but not at first making still life a subject on its own. Principally it was the Dutch in the sixteenth and seventeenth centuries who turned whole-heartedly to this manner. Painters of the qualities of Pieter Aertsen (1507–1573) – called *Lange Peer*, Long Peter – left behind some truly remarkable compositions that really pinpoint the beginning of still life studies. Aertsen's paintings are full of vigour, dramatic light and shade, and display a great sense of observation with the many different materials and surfaces with which he was concerned.

One of the most accomplished technicians in the rendering of the transparency of glass, the texture of fruit, fish and other surfaces was David de Heem (1570–1632). His works do not lay claim to public admiration; rather are they sincere and simple statements which show the artist's pleasure in seeing and

Table of Funeral Offerings on a Painted Coffin
British Museum, London

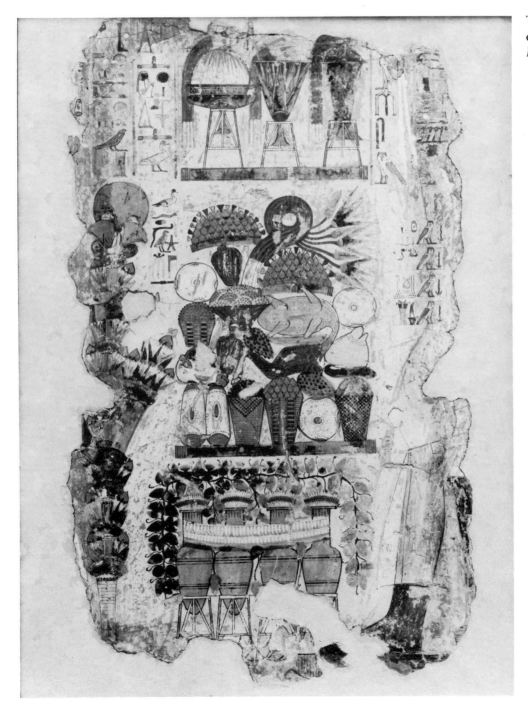

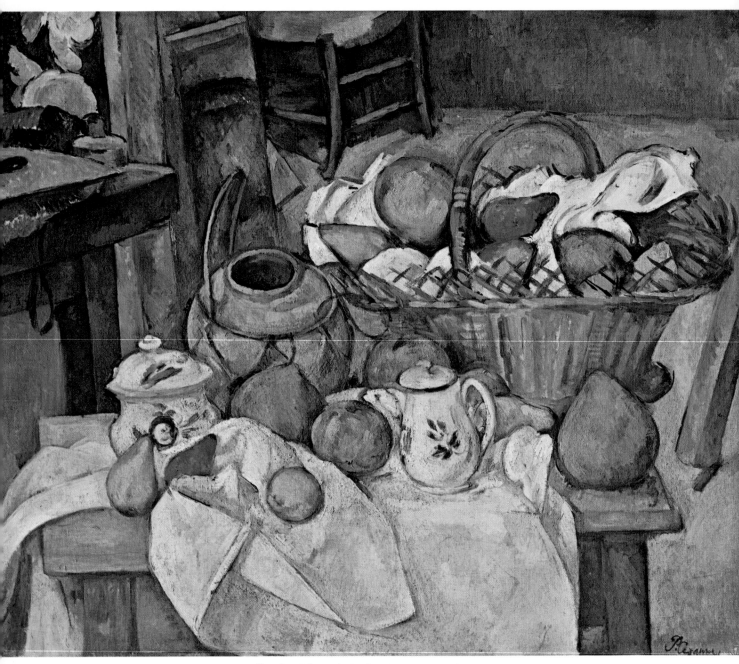

Cézanne: Still Life with Fruit Basket (*c* 1892–1893) 530 × 710 mm
Tate Gallery, London (page 88)

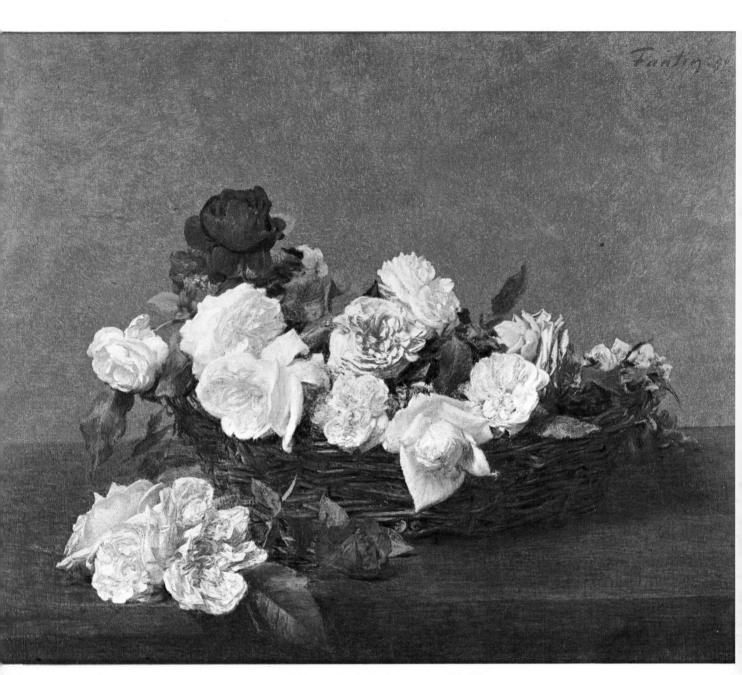

Fantin-Latour: Roses (1890) 489 × 603 mm
The National Gallery, London (page 100)

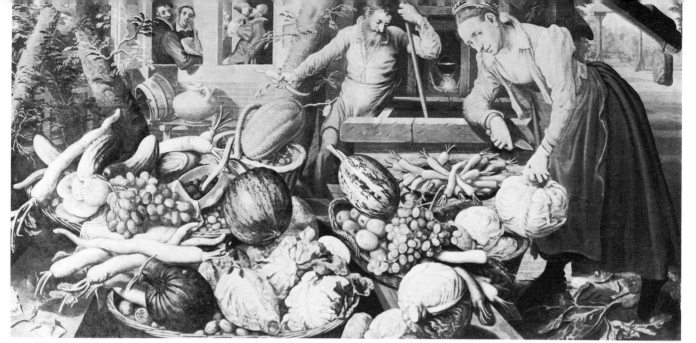

Aertsen: The Fruit and Vegetable Seller (1562)
835 × 1695 mm
Hallwylska Museum,
Stockholm

recording more than in trick performances. Pieter Claesz (1600–1661) has this same almost uncanny knack of producing the 'feel', the whole appearance of metal and glass.

That master of light and shade, Michelangelo Merisi, called Caravaggio after his birthplace (1573–1610), had a great flair for this subject. It is recorded that he turned to painting fruit and flowers 'being too poor to afford models' on his first arrival in Rome. Caravaggio was a revolutionary in paint. He was as determined to dispense with the 'antique' and the 'grand manner' as are any of the moderns. He wanted to go back to nature, to show things as they appeared in reality, not as if, through art, they had undergone a transfiguration.

If you are in Vienna, in the Pinakothek, one of the real off-beat gentlemen who is worth a look at is Giuseppe Arcimboldo (1533–1593). He built up strange fanciful portraits entirely from fruit and vegetable forms and there are also examples of a face made up of books, and a portrait of *John Calvin* composed of fishes and birds. Maybe there is some satirical significance with the last, probably intended to ridicule the hated heretic. Arcimboldo, it appears, was not only a painter but also Master of the Revels to the two German Emperors Maximilian II and Rudolf II.

In the same genre as still life are the *trompe l'oeil* productions of some painters. It is almost as though these pictures were deliberately created to deceive the eye. One such who occasionally painted in this way was Wallerant Vaillant (1623–1677) (*A Letter Rack* – Dresden Gallery). Like the French painter Jean Baptiste Chardin, he was interested in simple everyday items. Chardin (1699–1779) was possibly one of the most sensitive still life painters; his edges are soft; the light suffuses rather than strikes. Against the richness and excesses of his time in France, Chardin must have seemed an outcast. He probably made one of the most important pronouncements on still life, or for that matter any subject in painting. This was: 'It does not matter what you paint, it is how you paint it.' A truism that is well worth remembering and acting upon.

Nearer today the Post-Impressionist Paul Cézanne (1839–1906) can be seen turning his hand to still life with arrangements of fruit, kitchen utensils, and small statues. He does not attempt the true realism of the early Dutchmen but brings a new life and kick to the subject by exploring it with his cubist, solid approach.

Georges Braque takes this individual treatment even further and uses the objects with their colours and textures as jumping-off grounds for his exquisite arrangements of colour harmonies and tones.

A still life arrangement in your own studio can include practically anything: everyday objects of domestic use, fruit, vegetables, musical instruments. Backgrounds can be made from velvet drapes, netting, rough wood, or plain

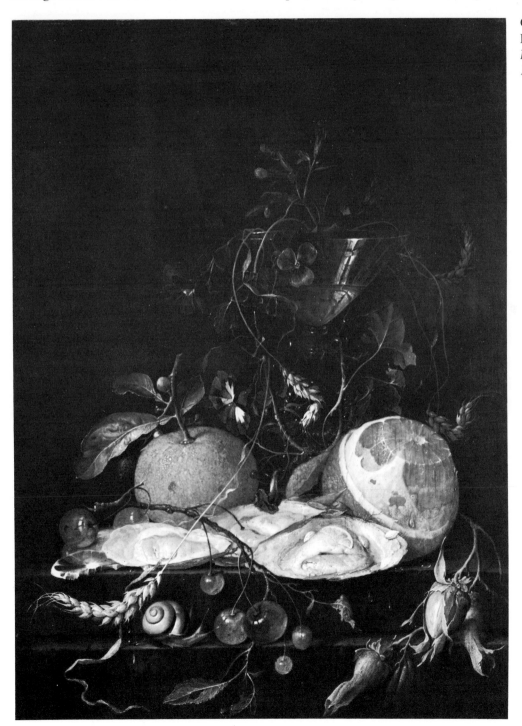

Caravaggio: Flowers and Fruit
Pinacoteca Ambrosiana, Milan

89

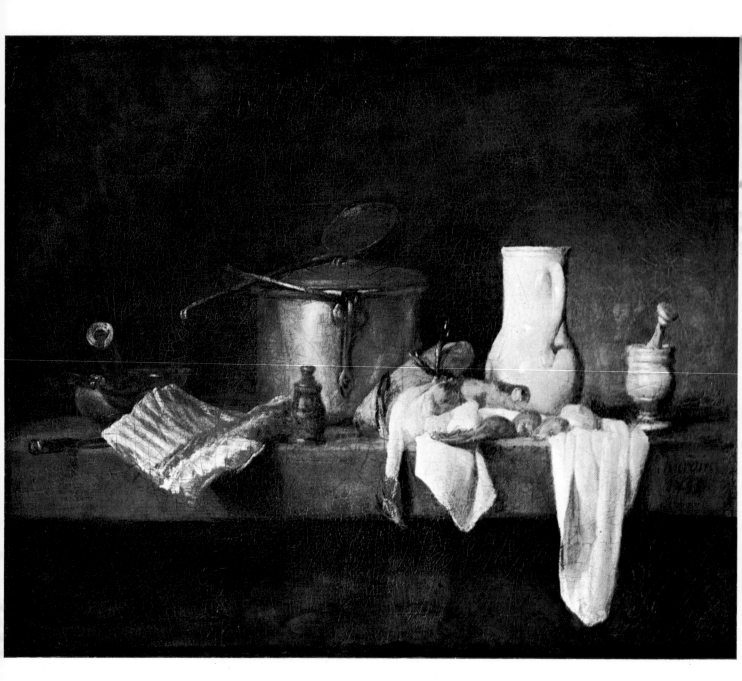

Chardin: A Kitchen Table
Museum of Fine Arts,
Boston, Mass., Gift of
Mrs Peter Chardon Brooks
(page 88)

Chardin was one of the
great masters of the gentle
statement. Note the
softness of the light which
leads to an absence of hard
edges, but brings out the
forms in a most convincing
manner.

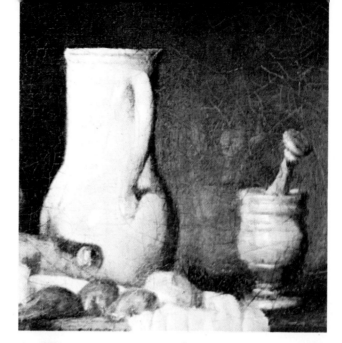

Chardin: A Kitchen Table

Right – top to bottom
The details show the
treatment of: the tall white
jug to the right: the napkin
just below it: the copper pot
and the joint of meat.

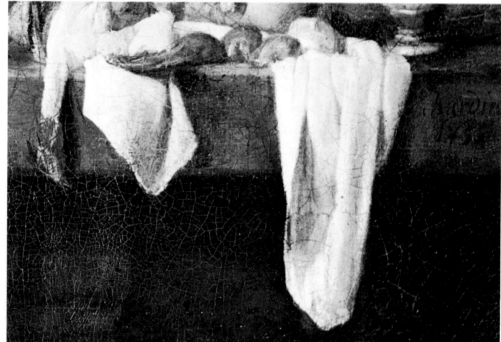

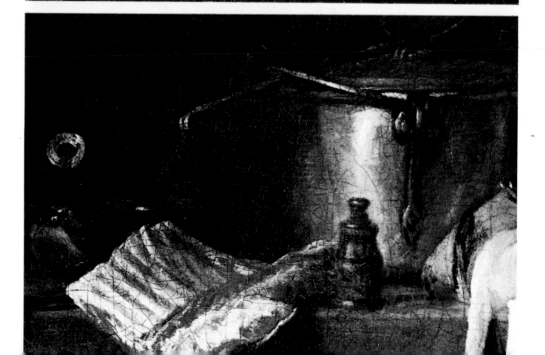

plaster walls. For the first composition, keep it simple, have perhaps just three or four objects of different materials and surface, so that there will be contrasts and textures to search out. A red earthenware jug, a pewter plate with two lemons; here you will have colour and the problem of achieving the different textures of the earthenware, the lemon skin and the metal.

In the preceding chapter there are some comments on composition, the relationship of the main object to the canvas and the use of symmetry and asymmetry. Broadly speaking for most compositions, whatever the subject, an asymmetrical arrangement is the better; it tends to provide interest and to lead the eye into the picture. Having arranged your group of objects, now concentrate on the lighting source. Two different light sources will obviously give two totally different pictures. Here is one of the values of still life as an aid to progress: the exact effects of light and shade can be studied and understood; the subtleties of reflected lights can be seen and the way in which modelling is

Claesz: Still Life with Drinking Vessels (1649)
635 × 524 mm
The National Gallery, London

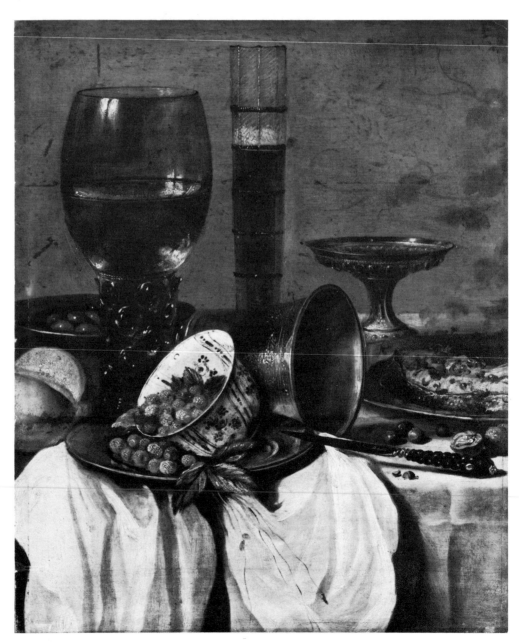

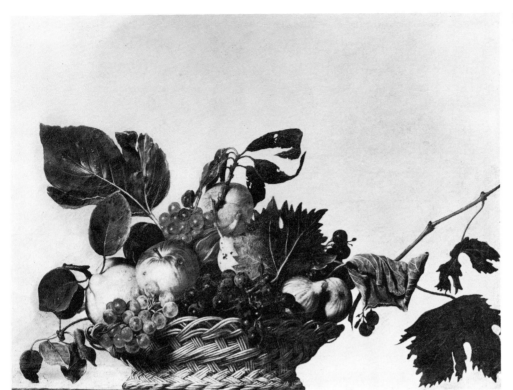

induced by highlight, half tone and shadow. It is easy to overlook reflected light and reflected colour: the lemons, for example, will throw their colour against the pewter plate, and if the lemon skins have a gloss they will probably pick up some of the glow from the earthenware jug.

Having blocked in your main objects, whether you are working in watercolour, acrylic or oils, the background should be painted in first. This rule applies not only to still life but also in general to all subjects.

With a simple subject such as this still life with the jug, lemons and plate, full attention can be given to each area. After the background, then work up the table on which the group stands, follow this with the jug, the plate and then the lemons. Do not be tempted to work away at any one particular part of the picture until that area is finished – if this is done it will be very difficult to maintain overall harmony as the painting proceeds. The painting of the background can be largely brought to a near finished state, but with the main objects leave accents of highlight and shade until right at the end.

When looking at a subject for the first time it is an aid to simplification if the eyes are half-closed. In this way much of the light is shut out and the objects resolve themselves down to their basic shapes. If these can be grasped and recorded the composition will very soon gain strength and register. All the time, remember that you are not truly trying to compete with the camera. Do not get bogged down with attempting to depict the minutiae of intricate details. Let the objects or scene before you act as a trigger to your own personal feeling for the subject.

A painting is the expression of the ideas that a painter has in his mind. Although much of painting is concerned with the representational, much of the

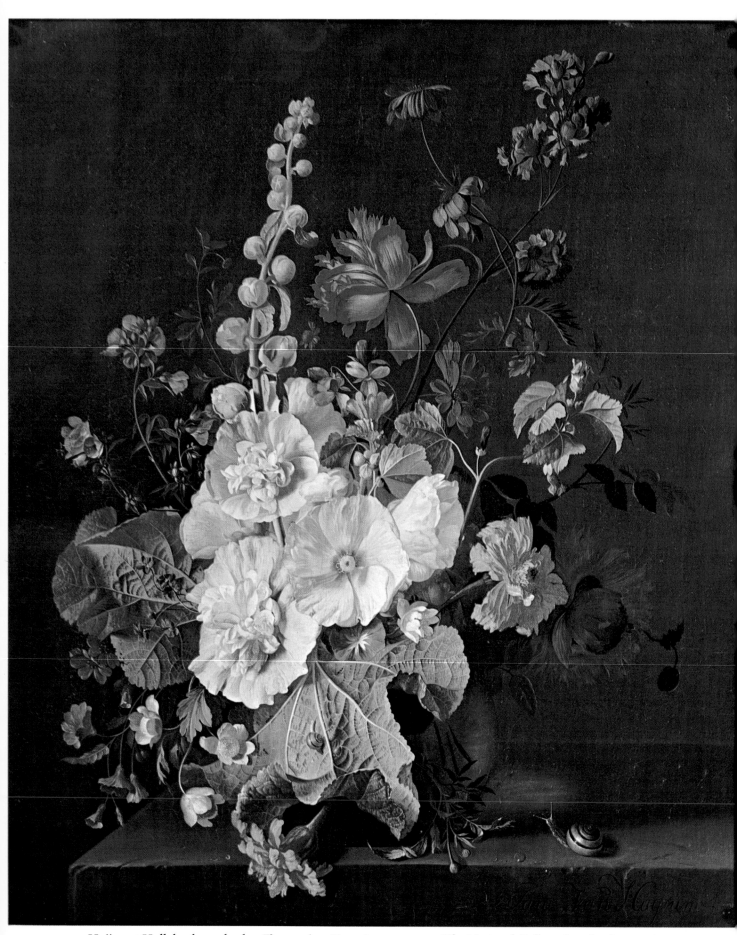

Huijsum: Hollyhocks and other Flowers in a Vase 621 × 523 mm *The National Gallery, London* (page 96)

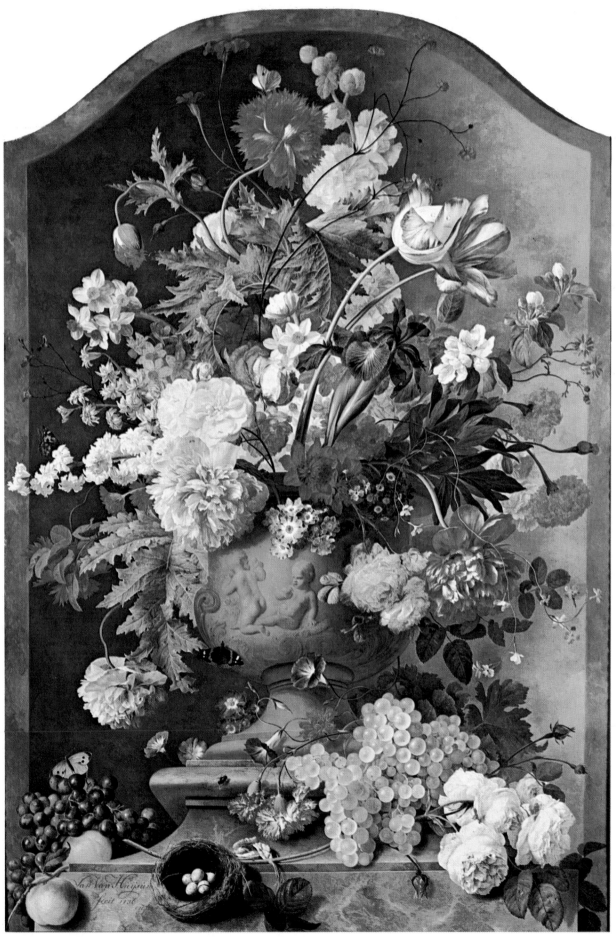

Huijsum: Flowers in a Terracotta Vase (1736–1737) 1335 × 915 mm *The National Gallery, London* (page 96)

small areas and individual relationships of form and colour are abstract in their effect. Colour harmony is a subtle matter and it can be appreciated in its simplest forms by still life studies.

The placing of marks of colour on to a surface has a pleasurable feeling quite apart from the finer points of building up a picture. The effect on the eye is not only mental, it is physical. There are reactions from the arrangements of colour against colour. As these tones and tints are sought for in the model they enter the mind and touch off individual responses for each of us. These responses then form up on the canvas and paper in front of us as a translation of the scene. Twenty people painting the same group of objects from the same viewpoint and with the same light source, will produce variants which will underline this infinity of the mind that governs the physical action. The creative thought is seizing upon the examples in front of it to form its own reflection of them.

Flowers

Very close to *Still Life* as a subject is that of *Flowers*. They are not quite the same, as there is a compulsion to finish flowers within a given time which there is not with still life. The inanimate objects will stay the same, but flowers will wither and will even change their positions in quite a short time, depending upon the light source, the temperature and time of day. The colours are so pure and strong that it needs practice to be able to apply them cleanly to give the full ring. As with still life, examples of flowers in art go back far in history. The painting of flowers first emerged as a subject in the Far East. In the seventh century some early Chinese painters dropped traditional subjects and used their exquisite refined brush-work to show flower and plant forms. The Japanese continued the poetical and sympathetic treatment of flowers. Not only did they paint them but they were often transferred to woodcuts, particularly by the great Hokusai, who worked during the latter part of the eighteenth century and on into the nineteenth.

In Europe, flower painting as a separate subject did not really become popular until the seventeenth and eighteenth centuries. In Holland one of the most accomplished flower painters was Jan Van Huijsum (1682–1749). At his best he showed a complete understanding of the very nature of flowers, while his colouring was refined and restrained. During his lifetime Van Huijsum was held in great esteem by his contemporaries. Many journeyed far to study his technique. Lavish praise was given to his meticulous finish, and he was held in veneration by connoisseurs, collectors and art historians. He was one of the first to paint flowers with a light background which was considered to be much more difficult than with a dark. John Ruskin wrote: 'The world is so old that there is no dearth of things first-rate: and life so short that there is no excuse for looking at things second-rate. Let us then go to Rubens for blending, and to Titian for quality of colour; to Veronese for daylight and Rembrandt for lamp-

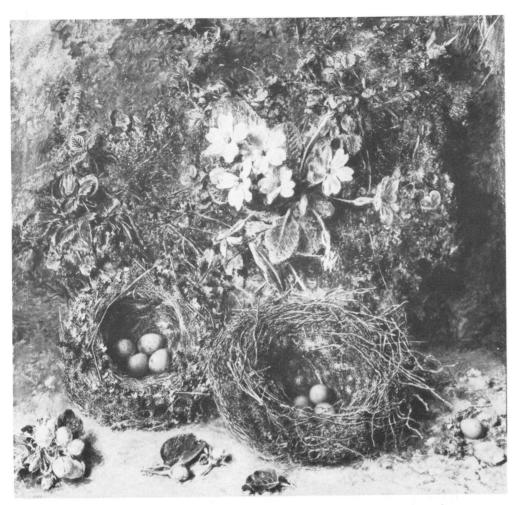

light; . . . and to Van Huijsum for precision. Any man is worthy of respect in his own rank who has pursued any truth or attainment with all his heart and strength.'

But what are the facts of much of Van Huijsum's work, particularly his later compositions? His flower groups were not painted as a whole from Nature but compiled from elaborate studies which he had made. This must be the case because all the blooms of the different flowers could not possibly be out at the same time. Compare the second of the Van Huijsum pictures with the first; this latter displays in truth a very artificial arrangement with objects like the bird's nest and the crisp hard edges; there is none of the depth of feeling as with the first picture, in which so beautifully sensed is the light and tone that it seems one could put one's fingers in amongst the flowers and feel their very substance.

If it is a question of complete and accurate recording, few can compete with William Holman Hunt (1790–1864) the Pre-Raphaelite. Again Ruskin spoke out and wrote: 'I am aware of no other pieces of art in modern days, at once so sincere and so accomplished.' Hunt is in fact an Impressionist; he did not employ outlines in his drawings; he applied his colour with little touches of the brush. Perhaps his worst fault, especially in his still life paintings, is his lack of design and composition. It seems he is so taken up with the problems of acute observation and detail that the remainder is overlooked.

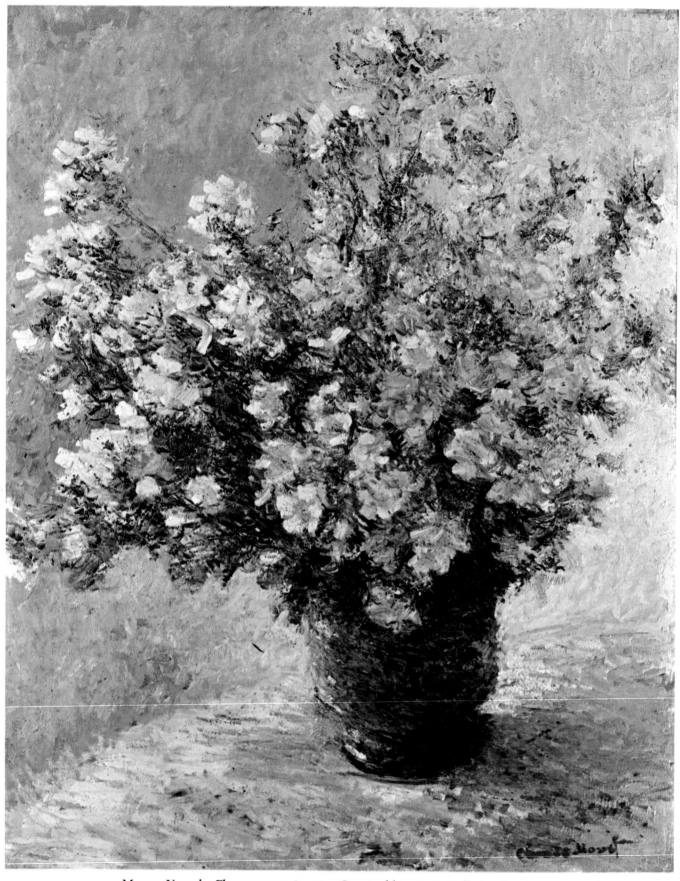

Monet: Vase des Fleurs 1000 × 810 mm *Courtauld Institute Galleries, London* (page 100)

Opposite. **Gauguin: Mandolin and Flowers** (1885) 610 × 510 mm *Louvre, Paris* (page 100)

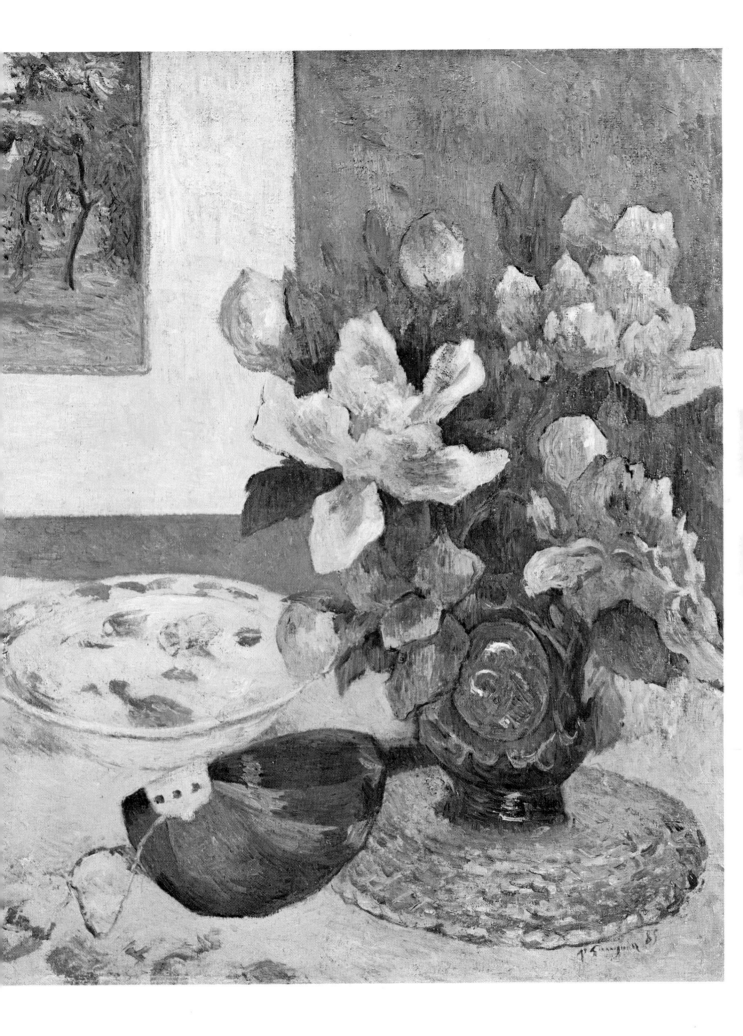

Van Huijsum may have had the acclaim of the world in his own time but for many tastes today he falls behind the sheer quality and genius of Ignace Henri Jean Theodore Fantin-Latour (1836–1904). Fantin-Latour's father was a well known pastellist from Metz and his mother a Russian. For a time he studied with Lecoq de Boisbaudran, the famous teacher of drawing based on memory, and later at the École des Beaux-Arts, and for a short time with Couture. He was a great craftsman and spent years of his life copying the old masters in the Louvre. When he painted flowers the one quality that comes out is his love of the beautiful blooms, his sympathy with the softness of the petals, the ephemeral colours. He does not go for dramatic light and shade. His canvases have a gentle quality of that light the French call *crépuscule*. In contrast to Fantin-Latour's work is a flower painting by the Impressionist, Claude Monet (1840–1926). To Monet, flowers are a challenge to his control of colour. The blooms become notes from which he can weave an idealistic harmony. The bunch of flowers evokes an orchestral rhythm.

Two examples in different veins are compositions by Paul Gauguin (1848–1903) and Vincent Van Gogh (1853–1890) which can be seen in the National Gallery. Gauguin, a Parisian, the son of a Breton and Peruvian Creole, was at first an amateur, a once-a-week Sunday painter. His final inspiration was to come from the heady climate of Tahiti and his colour is redolent with his own fiery character. Flowers as painted by Van Gogh, although put on with his readily recognisable staccato brush-work, have an unsuspected sympathy.

In painting flowers do not go for photographic realism; it is much more important to catch the characteristics of the various blooms. Get hold of the basic shape of the bloom cup or petal arrangement. Note how the blooms and buds sit on the stems. See how the leaves are set, pick up the textures. Certain flowers have a definite feel about them. Sunflowers are huge and tend to be ungainly compared with the gentle quality of roses. Tulips exhibit a form of classic grace with their clear cut stems and leaves. Flower painting is not an art that can succeed by casual attempt, it really calls for quite deliberate thought and will be a trial of skill and sensitivity to enable success to be complete.

Often pure knife painting can succeed where the more laboured use of a brush loses. The use of a knife demands boldness and breadth of treatment. It makes the user go for clean strong colour and also use plenty of it. Before making a start, however, a safety measure can be to produce several small 'thumb nail' sketches of different arrangements of the chosen subject, also varying colour treatments. These will help you decide as to the best course and will act as guides for the actual painting. A knife painting, as with a brush, needs only the skeleton of the subject indicated. The lines are to be taken as the merest guides and should not be restrictive for the actual painting. If possible several different-shaped knives should be used, as in this way variety of stroke and texture can be maintained.

First of all put in the background. It is probably best to keep this to a fairly gentle stroke without too great an impasto as this will allow for the strength to be kept for the main subject and the foreground. Pick up the colour cleanly from the palette and try to bring the strokes of the knife down in the right place straightaway so that they do not have to be gone over again. Paint put on with a knife stroke that has to be touched a second time loses its sparkle and life. After the background, go for the boards on which the plant stands. Here greater variation of texture can be used, the knife blade point can be wriggled through the paint to simulate wood grains. After this put in the shadow and the pot. Look for the different tones on the pot, the highlit area, half tone, shade and reflected light. When the pot is finished turn the attention to the leaves, all the time bearing in mind variety of stroke. Painting knives, as with brushes, can be held in several different ways and they can also be pulled up, dragged down, slid sideways, or lifted suddenly to raise the paint, each time producing varieties of texture. The real test of the ability comes when the flowers are reached. If the colour is at all dirty the painting will fail. To achieve the purity of tint in a rose, the fiery red of a poppy, the richness of an iris, calls for the ultimate in paint handling. As the picture proceeds and comes closer to completion, stand back more and more and look well before each stroke is made. It is much better to leave a painting while it is still fresh and lively and not quite finished than to go on too long and work the life right out of it.

Landscapes

Probably for most painters landscape painting provides the greatest pleasure. It is something which is at the same time simple and complicated. There is no nice cosy studio with controlled light and static groups. A landscape is a vital thing. The wind will cause trees to move, grass to undulate like a swell at sea, scudding clouds will cast their chasing shadows across the hills, and worst of all the light source will move. It is quite extraordinary how different a scene that was started at ten in the morning will look by the time it gets to midday. Perhaps this is the reason why some conscientious specialists will return again and again to the same scene and work each day for about half an hour so that the light source will be as near as possible the same.

The composition of a landscape is fascinating and is a problem with which it is quite legitimate to use artistic licence. A view may be selected and then it is found that some trees appear slightly awkward, a building is at a wrong angle, a bend of a river is not quite right. Here is the time to use a sketchbook. Sort out the main bones of the composition and use a little gentle rearrangement. It may be a help to hold your hands up to roughly frame the view or carry with you a piece of card with a rectangle cut in it that can be used as a simple view-finder to isolate what you want to paint from the rest of the landscape.

To start with, it is better to keep to a horizontal rectangle for your canvas or paper. So-called portrait or upright rectangles can be awkward shapes to fill happily with a landscape.

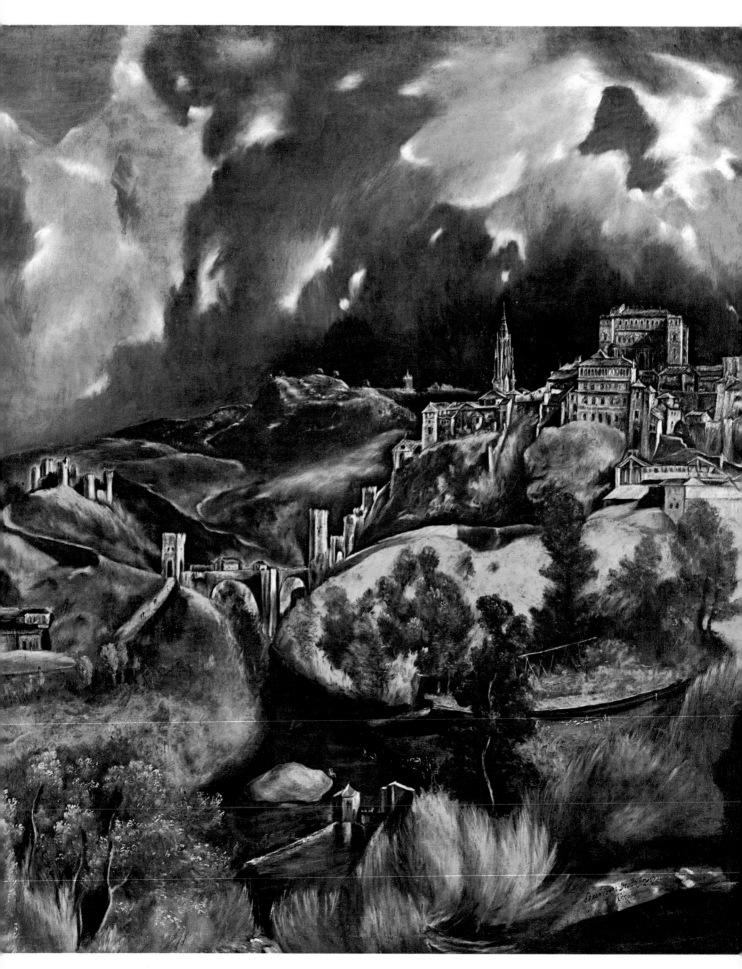

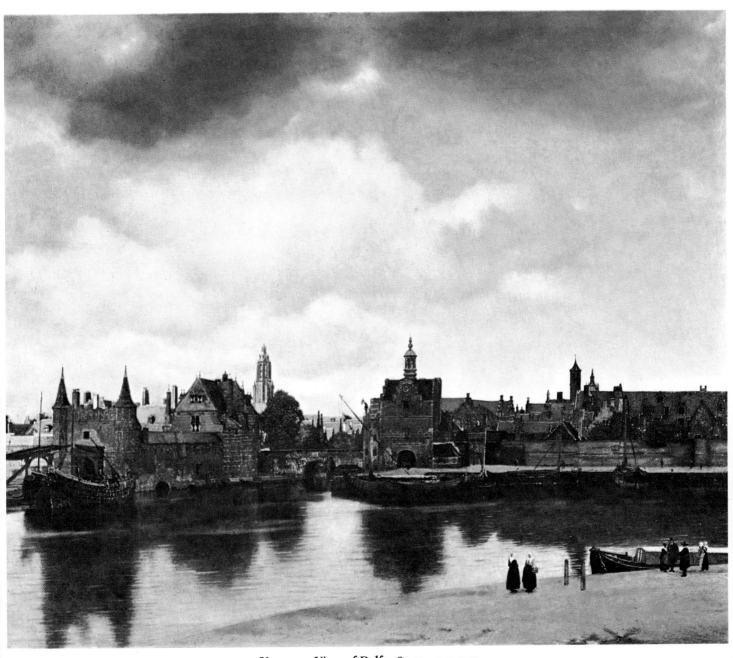

Vermeer: View of Delft 985 × 1175 mm
Mauritshuis, The Hague (page 108)

Opposite. **El Greco: Toledo** (1597–1599) 1210 × 1060 mm
Metropolitan Museum of Art, New York.
Bequest of Mrs H. O. Havemeyer, 1929.
The H. O. Havemeyer Collection (page 108)

A landscape is really a gathering together of individual objects and areas. There will be plants and flowers, still life objects, people, in a setting which can be composed of buildings, trees, rocks, grass, and nearly always with an appreciable area of sky in the background. But there is also another quality, which is depth. In a studio work this is not of great concern but outside it is all important if some sense of realism is to be achieved. To a certain degree the attaining of this depth or recession in a picture of a landscape can be got by the use of perspective. Lines of telegraph posts walking away into the distance, a road that disappears over a hill, relationship of buildings at different positions, these will all help. But alone they are not enough. This feeling of recession has got to be tackled by the use of colour as well.

Colour perspective is more reliable than linear perspective. Green grassy hills, which in the foreground are pungent and bright with strong yellows, when they are viewed from the distance appear pale blue-mauve; strong brown gnarled tree-trunks appear almost ethereal in blues and greys. The broadest rule is that the distance will tend to be light-toned and cool, the foreground strong-toned and warm. The sky will be an area of light tone over the land although this theory is completely upset in the winter when heavy green-grey storm clouds back up behind a snow-laid landscape.

Probably there can be no better preparation for such painting as a long quiet walk through the countryside, searching with the eyes for the colours, reflections, shapes and forms. Stop now and then when the eye is caught and make a note in your sketchbook. Turner built up his capacity for his wonderful bravura displays of atmospheric landscape from the understanding of countless hundreds of noted landscape incidents.

When tackling a landscape, in whatever medium, as with still life or flowers, start with the area furthest away. This will almost always be the sky, and the colour of the sky is for many one of the hardest to estimate accurately. It will not just be a matter of French ultramarine and white. Depending on the time of day, the season of the year, whether it is deep country or an industrial scene, that seemingly blue sky will need touches of crimson and yellow ochre to bring it to the correct tint. White clouds will nearly always have a slight tone. Clouds have their own special shapes, some formations mean rain, some wind, some setting fair. Generally speaking, clouds are crisp on the top and soft underneath. As the sky falls to the horizon, the blue tone will become paler and absorbed in a warm pinky, yellow-grey.

The distant hills in places like Connemara can be as purple as Paul Henry painted them. In Scotland they will be more of a steely blue.

Trees in a landscape need careful observation. They all have their own particular characteristics, the way the bole is set in the ground, the angle of the branches, the massing of the foliage. The Pre-Raphaelite painters like John Everett Millais and William Holman Hunt may have attempted to put in every leaf, but this does not necessarily project a sense of realism. A Pre-Raphaelite painting which has everything in focus, as in *A Hireling Shepherd* by Holman

Hunt (Tate Gallery), gives a sense of unreality. The human eye has comparatively little depth of focus and could not in a single glance see a landscape in this manner.

Painting a landscape, first and foremost, after the selection of the view and its components, is a matter of simplification and analysis. Half close the eyes and at once intricate collections of trees become a coherent mass. Complicated architectural details are shown in their basic simple forms. Block in these main masses first and then judge where the accents of light, shade and greater detail can best be put.

Landscape provides the painter with one of his strongest challenges. Very seldom will the ideal composition present itself or will the ideal weather be present. There are two approaches: one is to make a number of sketches and build these into the picture in the comfort of the studio; the second is to rough it out against the elements with the scene in front of you all the time. As to which will give the better result is a personal matter. Painters over the last three or four hundred years have worked in both manners and produced masterpieces.

During the time of the Italian Renaissance there were practically no landscapes painted as subjects by themselves. Often elaborate and beautifully executed scenes were included as backgrounds for religious pictures and paintings of mythology. The Renaissance influence spread itself to Spain and there one dedicated artist not only gave a bright shaft of inspiration to religious subjects but also painted scenes, particularly of the place where he lived. El Greco (1541–1614) was born in Crete and his first introduction to painting was working on icons in the Byzantine tradition. Later he travelled to Venice, where he is supposed to have studied with Titian, and was influenced by Bassano and Tintoretto, and possibly Correggio. Later he went to Rome but, sickened by the intrigue, left and travelled to Spain and Toledo. To look at his *View of Toledo* and to realize that it was painted about three hundred and fifty years ago brings astonishment. El Greco creates here a marvellously simplified landscape against a stormy shattered sky. His treatment of trees, vegetation and buildings provides object lessons even today. The colour relationships of the sunlit scene against the sky are emotional and full of power. He has caught a moment of elemental atmosphere.

Sixty years before El Greco was born, in Germany – which at that time was an intricate collection of separate states, a part of Europe which until then had had little influence from the Renaissance – there was born Albrecht Altdorfer (1480–1538). He was to become one of the leading figures of the German Renaissance and the Danube school. Some of the technical advances of the Italian Renaissance may have been absorbed but the spiritual content did not touch the minds of those taken up with the Reformation. Altdorfer had a very particular contribution to add to landscape painting. He was, and still is, one of the masters of filling a scene with a vast number of figures, *The Battle of Arbela* is among the most remarkable pictures ever painted. Note the subtle repetition

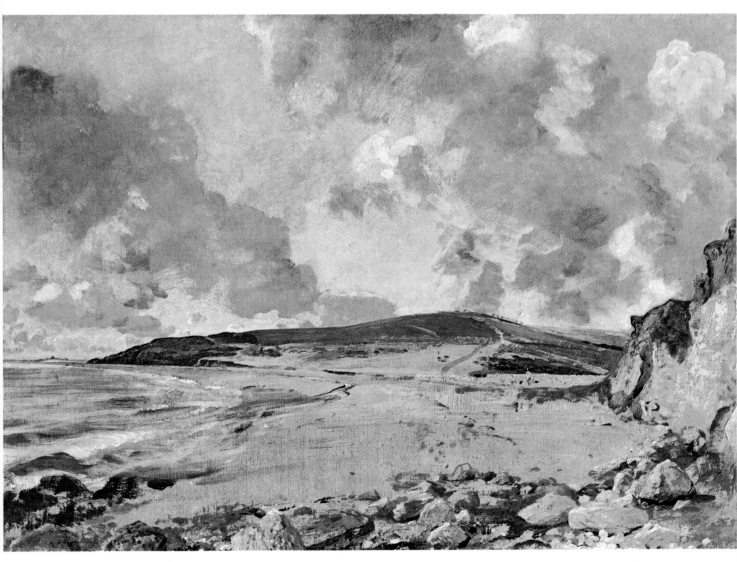

Constable: Weymouth Bay 533 × 749 mm
The National Gallery, London (page 109)

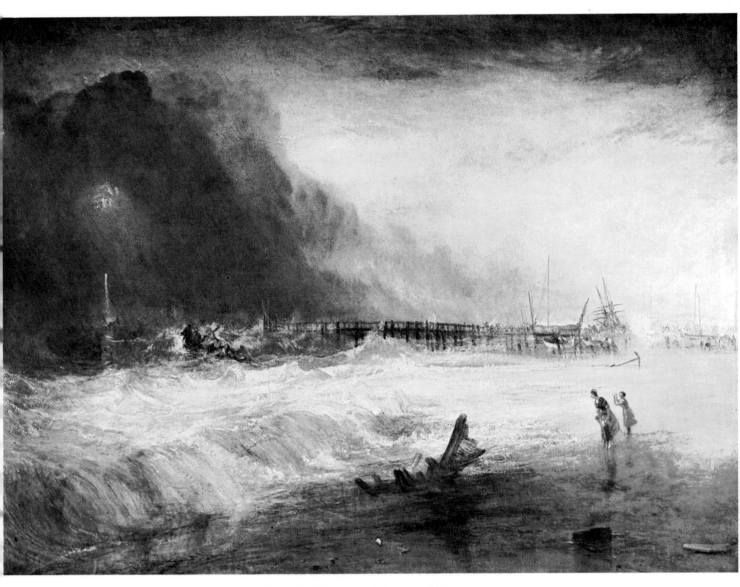

Turner: Vessel in Distress off Yarmouth 800 × 1200 mm
Victoria and Albert Museum, London (page 112)

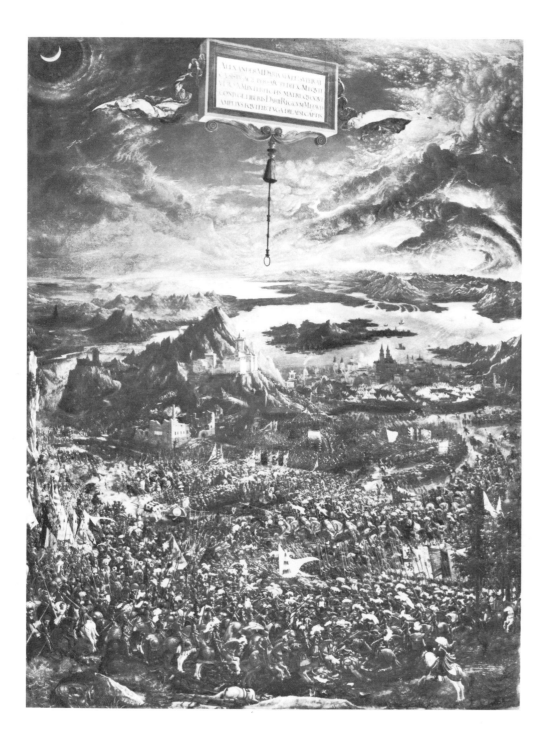

of the shape of the regiments of soldiers and cavalry in the contorted sky.

Whereas El Greco and Altdorfer were to a large extent isolated examples of genius in this genre, the Dutch school of the seventeenth century had many masters of landscape and their influence has been considerable, especially on the East Anglian school and even on painters of nineteenth-century France. The celebrated Jan Vermeer (1632–1675), although he is largely known for his exquisite interiors, with paintings like *View of Delft* discloses supreme understanding of landscape. The composition is not too formal, the handling of the water and the reflections is faultless, but perhaps most of all he anchors down his subject by catching local atmosphere as being in Holland and nowhere else. But foremost amongst the Dutch landscape painters must be Meindert Hobbema

(1638–1709). His *The Avenue, Middelharnis* is one of the most interesting landscapes from the point of view of composition. Here he deliberately rides over the accepted use of asymmetry and uses a near perfect symmetry. The long avenue is centrally placed, even the lines of the trees are all on the axis, yet the picture is full of interest from the figure working in the field in the right foreground to the little group of buildings and the distant tower; the eye is taken into the picture by the clever use of figures in the Avenue itself. The sky is most sensitively painted and it can be seen how Hobbema's work must have been a strong influence on painters like Crome and Cotman. The Dutch, besides handling landscape with skill, were equally at home with the sea, in particular the Van de Velde family gave much to this subject. William the Younger was probably the most skilled, and not only was competent with sea and sky but could paint the elaborate shipping of his time with accuracy.

The Dutch may have given landscape painting the quality of standing as a subject in its own right, but it was most truly liberated by John Constable (1776–1837) and Joseph Mallord William Turner (1775–1851). Constable, born at East Bergholt in Suffolk, set out at first to paint portraits but very soon turned his powers to landscape and he gave it a sense of realistic atmosphere. His meadows were damp with dew; his trees were convincing; his storm clouds were ready to drop their downpour. In *Weymouth Bay* can be felt the freshness of the channel wind blowing in across the sea. There is a wonderful sense of space with the open beach. In his own time Constable did not receive the recognition he should have in England, but when he showed *The Hay Wain* in France there was immediate triumph. Constable, in fact, was one of Ruskin's blind spots, for the critic supported Turner but more or less ignored Constable.

Turner, the son of a barber in Covent Garden, was an early starter and is reputed by the age of fourteen to have been earning his living selling his drawings. Probably no artist ever worked harder than Turner. He produced literally thousands of drawings, watercolours and oils. He travelled all over England and much of Europe. As he went he must have fed his mind from the scenes he saw, the fast changing landscapes, the effects of weather, all this built up in him until later in his life he painted pictures that were the very essence of elemental atmosphere. The winds, the mists, the showers, the glare of sunlight were all in Turner's brush. He gloried in the violence of sea and sky and in another mood caught the poetry of a moisture-soaked landscape steaming under the hot rays of the returning sun.

The French Impressionists in the nineteenth century brought a revolution to the whole of picture-making. The concept of composition and subject was fresh, and particularly with landscape they had something new to say. The principals were Claude Monet (1840–1926), Camille Pissarro (1830–1903) and Alfred Sisley (1840–1899). Sisley with his *L'Abreuvoir* is making a simple personal statement on the snowy scene in front of him. Note how he masses all the main components and how delicately any sense of detail is indicated. This

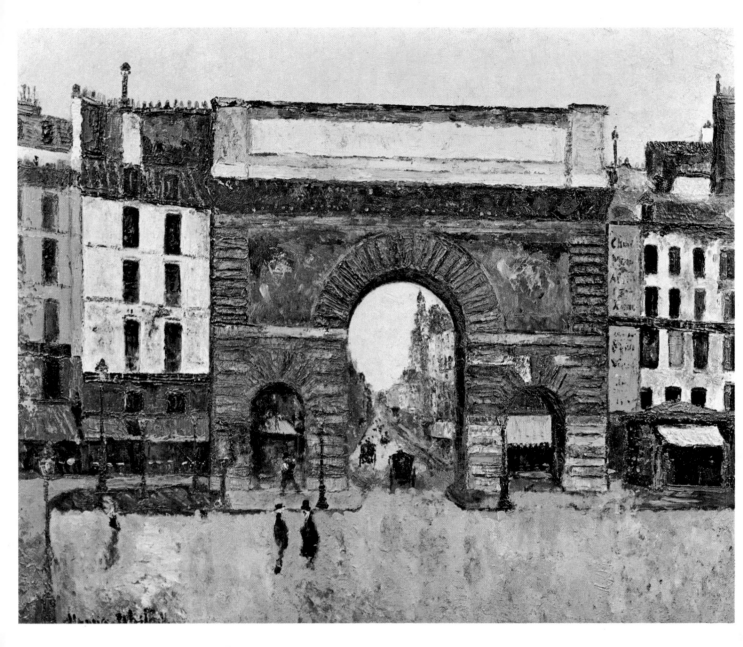

Utrillo: La Porte Saint Martin
Tate Gallery, London

The spontaneity of the
brushwork has captured the
atmosphere. Note the
simplicity of treatment with
the buildings and the
suggestion of surface texture.

Utrillo: La Porte Saint Martin

Top right. Details of roof
and windows from top
left-hand of picture.

Below, left and right.
The details show the
treatment of the main arch
and of the two figures in the
foreground.

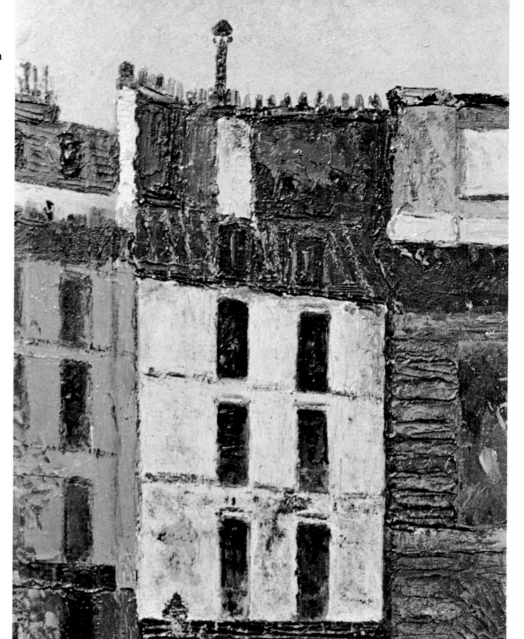

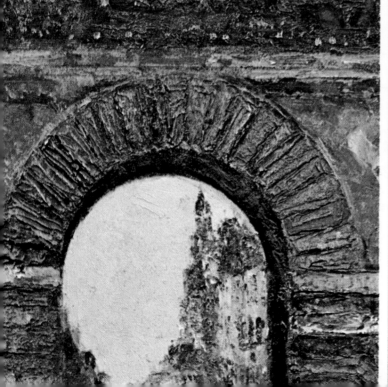

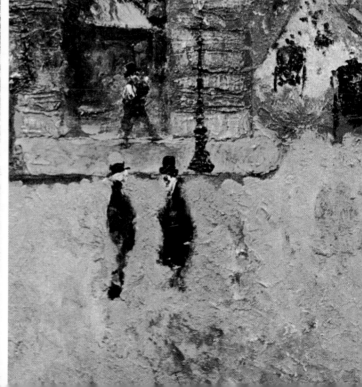

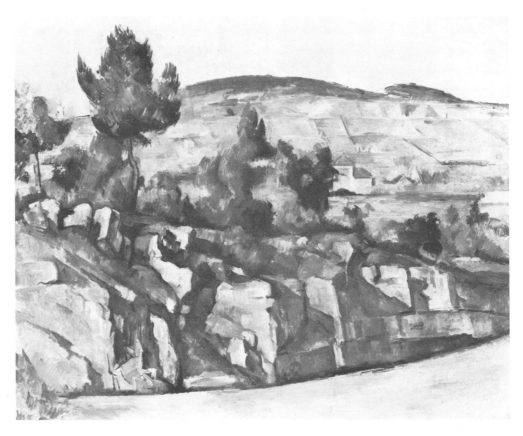

is far away from the powerful manner of Paul Cézanne, in whose *Rocky Landscape near Aix-en-Provence* the cubist influence can clearly be seen. Of his own works Cézanne said: 'I have not tried to reproduce nature, I have represented it.' Vincent Van Gogh was another contemporary of the Impressionists

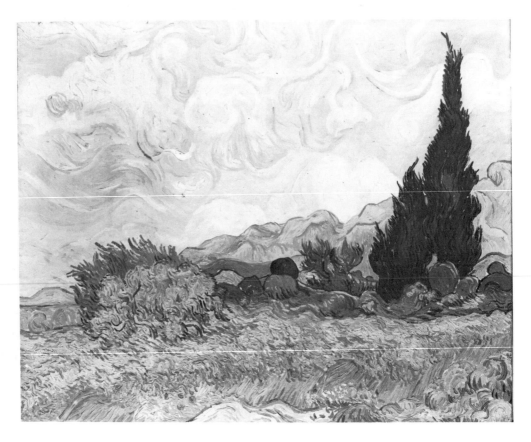

and it is of interest to compare his *Cornfield with Cypresses* with the picture by Cézanne and that by Sisley. Three distinct handlings of landscapes being produced at about the same time. Probably few painters have such thoroughly distinctive brush-work as Van Gogh, and a study of one of his pictures can be instructive in the handling of paint strokes and bright colours interplayed together, the whole full of seething virile strength.

That landscape can be a highly imaginative exercise has been shown by a number of painters in recent years. Stanley Spencer, the mystic, who lived in Cookham, sometimes took himself away from his religious subjects and produced pictures like *Rickett's Farm, Cookham Dene*, an accurately observed

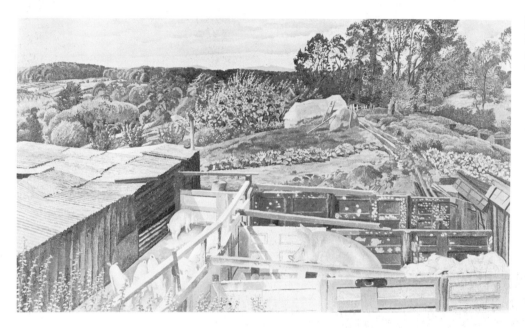

Spencer: Rickett's Farm,
Cookham Dene (1938)
650 × 1150 mm
Tate Gallery, London

landscape with almost Pre-Raphaelite detail and an unusual foreground with the pigs in their styes. Paul Nash with his *Dead Sea* gives what must be one of the most deeply moving scenes by a war artist. Here is the forceful rendering of the effects of the Battle of Britain which lie splayed out with the rhythm of some unknown ocean. Many things can combine to produce success with a landscape, whether it is of open country, of a village, or towns. Perhaps when a painter can strike within himself some creative poetry, some individual vision, he finds satisfaction for himself and his talent is seen. John Piper, whose creative work has included stained glass, theatrical design, and draughtsmanship and painting of a high order, often can treat the most ugly and distressing subject with sensitivity and can lift it from its context so that even a ruin has a dignity and beauty.

The industrial scene has attracted very few artists. L. S. Lowry, however, living up in the industrial north, has caught the sombre grey atmosphere, the old stained buildings, the teeming streets, and the towering belching factory chimneys. He has peopled his inimitable scenes with tiny folk that scamper about their business or stand and jaw. There is a feeling of Pieter Brueghel the Elder, but most of all here is a true creative individual at work.

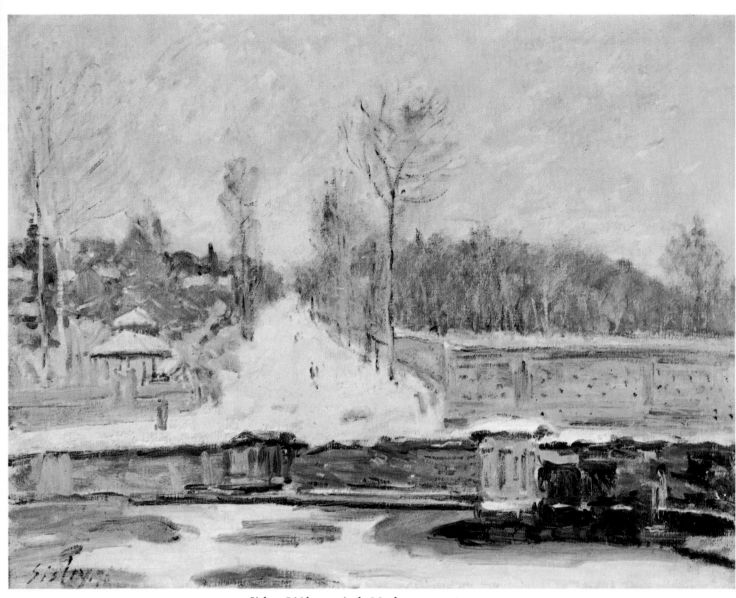

Sisley: **L'Abreuvoir de Marley** 495 × 654 mm
The National Gallery, London (page 112)

Opposite. **De Hooch: A Musical Party** (1677) 835 × 685 mm
The National Gallery, London (page 117)

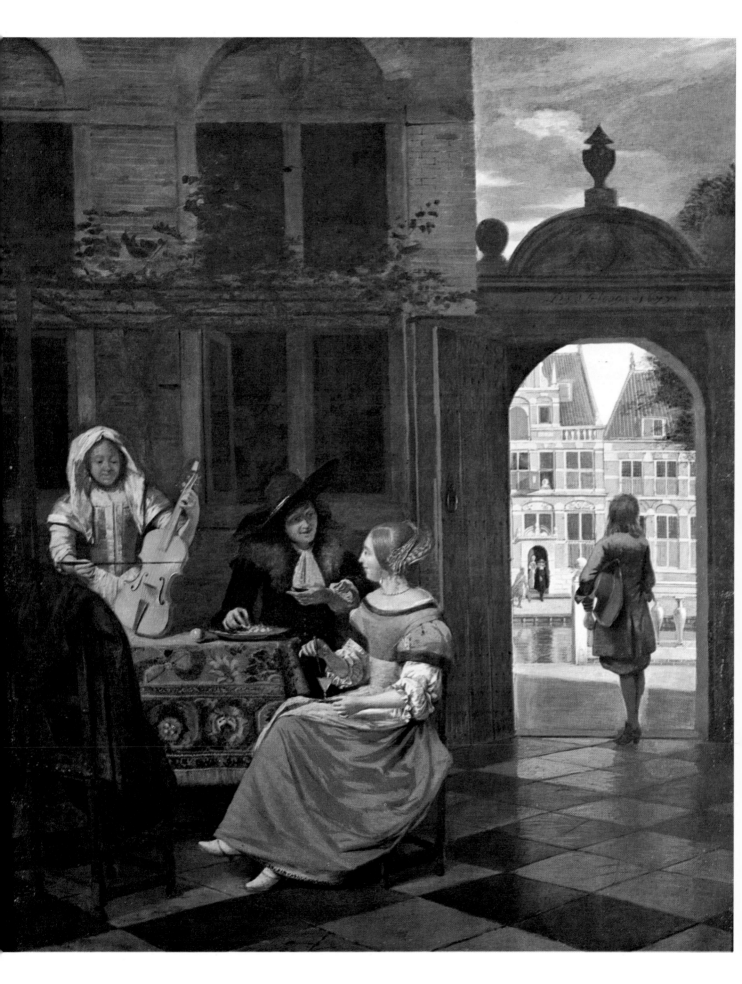

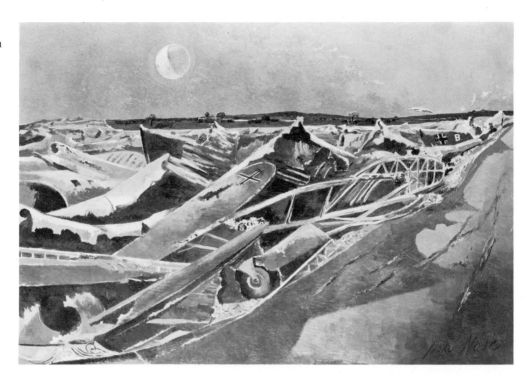

Right. **Paul Nash: Dead Sea**
(1940–1941) 1000 × 1500 mm
Tate Gallery, London

Below. **Piper: All Saints
Chapel, Bath** 420 × 550 mm
Tate Gallery, London

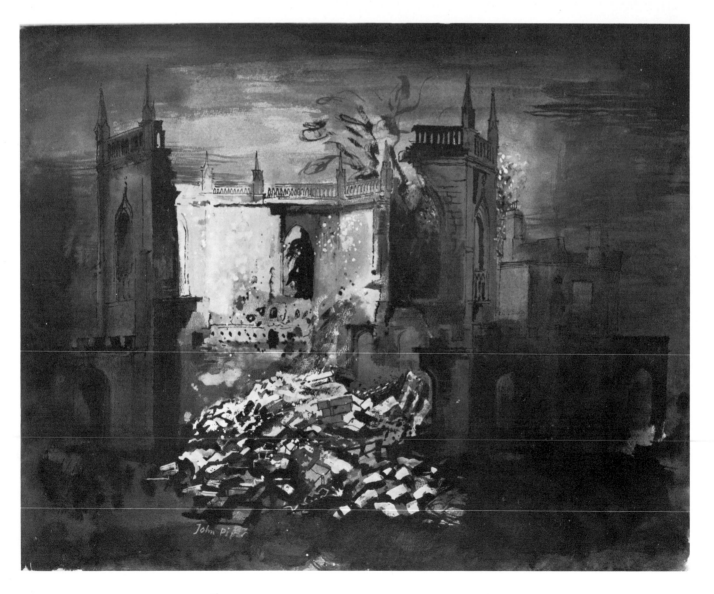

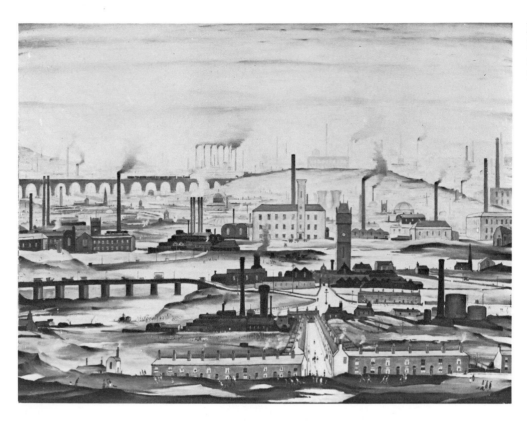

Interiors

The painting of an interior has a fascination of its own. One of the most difficult points is to learn to judge the tone values correctly. All too often one sees pictures of the interiors of churches and other buildings which fail to give the impression of being inside. Generally this is because the tone values of the walls are too dark or too light and are not related to their light sources. In some ways interior painting is similar to still life, as the viewpoint can be selected and the light source in some cases will be constant. Here again, the Dutch school of the seventeenth century produced a number of men who were masters of this subject. Pieter de Hooch was one who had an almost magical control of an interior. He often used devices of open doorways that gave on to courtyards, that showed other openings. These compositional manoeuvres ensured that the eye was not only drawn into the picture but explored it thoroughly. De Hooch's paintings are full of careful detail and immaculate perspective. In contrast to him was Peter Saenredam, who chose as his principal subjects the cool simple interiors of the Dutch churches. In *Church at Assendelft* (Amsterdam, Rijksmuseum) can be noted his sensitive handling of architecture and beautiful tone control. It is a very long step from this quiet piece of dignity to *The Night Café* by Van Gogh. The use of the bright red walls and the haze round the lamps produces a pulsing hot atmosphere. The slumped figures around the tables, the open space, evokes perfectly the scene of a small café at just after midnight when the main habitués have gone home.

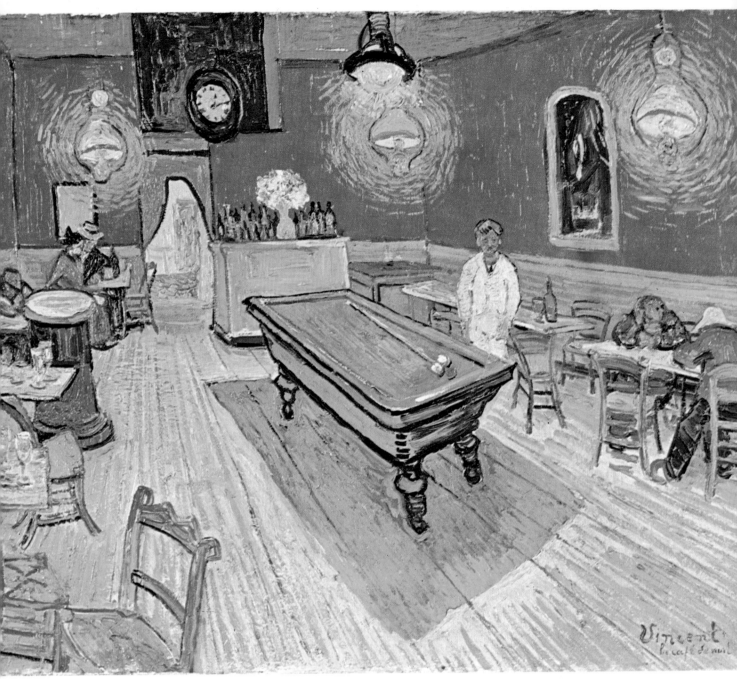

Van Gogh: The Night Café on the Place Lamartine, Arles (1888) 700 × 890 mm
Yale University Art Gallery, New Haven. Bequest of Stephen Carlton Clark (page 117)

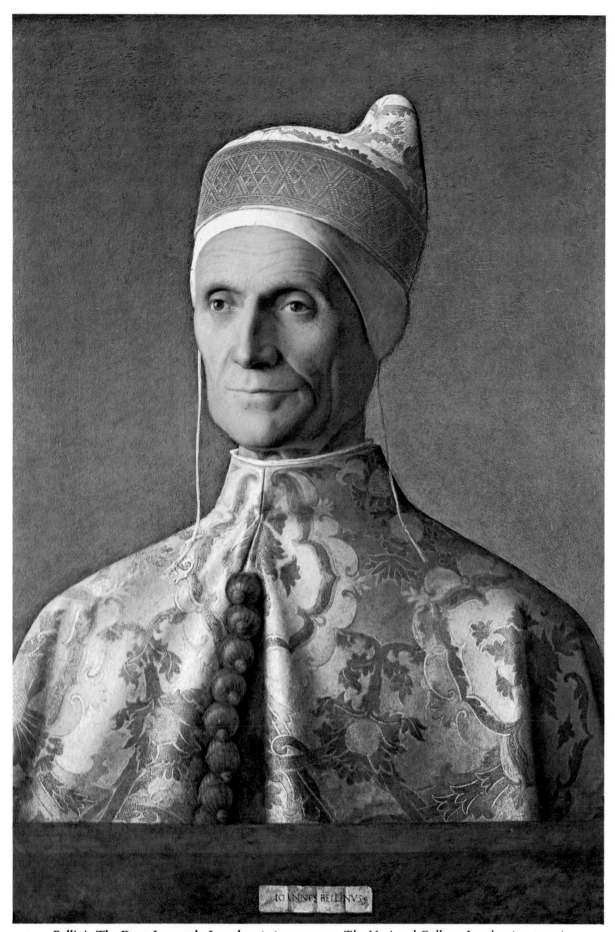

IOANNES BELLINVS

Bellini: The Doge Leonardo Loredan 616 × 451 mm *The National Gallery, London* (page 124)

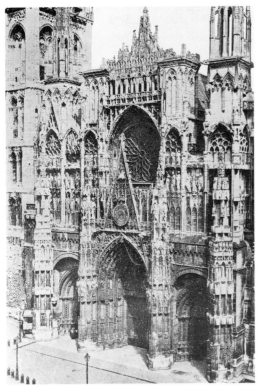

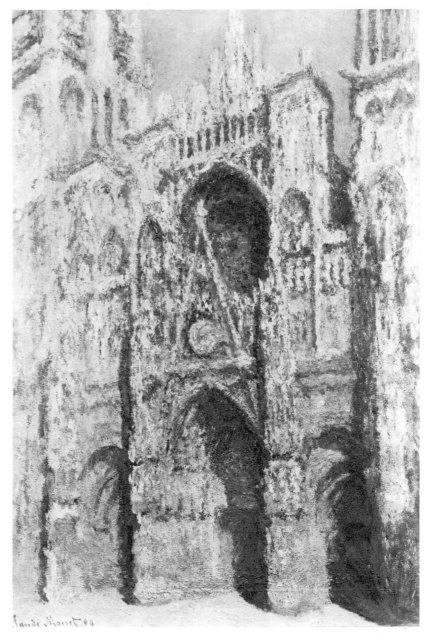

Examples of artist's licence
Compare the three paintings
and actual photographs.

**Claude Monet: Rouen Cathedral,
Full Sunshine**
Louvre, Paris

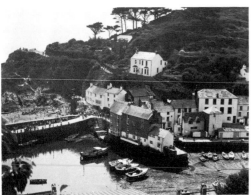

Oscar Kokoscha: Polperro, Cornwall
Tate Gallery, London

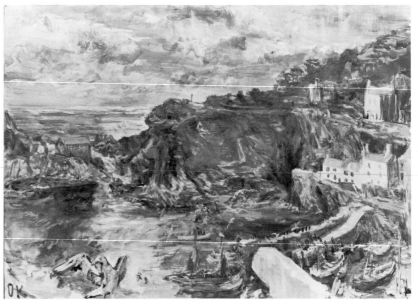

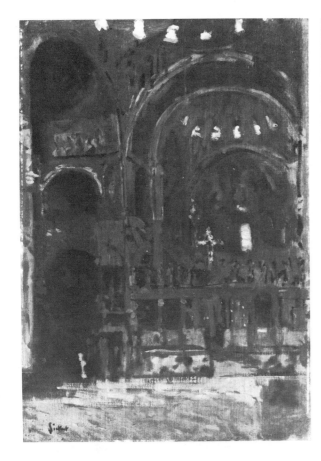

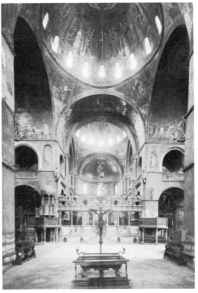

Walter Richard Sickert: Interior
of St Mark's, Venice
Tate Gallery, London

Portraits

The tackling of a portrait is best left until some considerable experience has
been gained in the handling of paint. The human head and figure are two of the
most complex problems for the painter. First, it is necessary to have some
understanding of anatomy, of the bone structure under the skin. A model when
sitting may look fairly static but even when calmly posed, quite considerable
changes can take place, a limb may sag and the colouring of the face can be
affected by temperature, by straining to hold the pose or by temperament.
Preliminary work should be comprehensive sketches, first in line and then in
tones, probably with charcoal or a soft Conté crayon. Studies can be made of
the individual features, the eyes, ears, nose, lips. In the case of the eye, note the
curves of the eyelids, the shape of the tear-duct. See the shape of the pupil and
iris. The lips have more subtleties in their curves than can be guessed until an
attempt is made to paint them. Look at the construction of the nose, the position
of the lobes of the nostrils. And perhaps most of all observe carefully the shape
of the face, the outline of the three-quarter view or profile. Many, on beginning
a portrait, try to seek safety in working away with fine detail at a particular
area. This is quite wrong. Approach portrait painting as you would a landscape
or a still life. Half close the eyes. Resolve everything down to simple basic
shapes, and put these in with a broad treatment. Once these are correct, then
you will be in a position to give an accent or a lift to a particular feature.

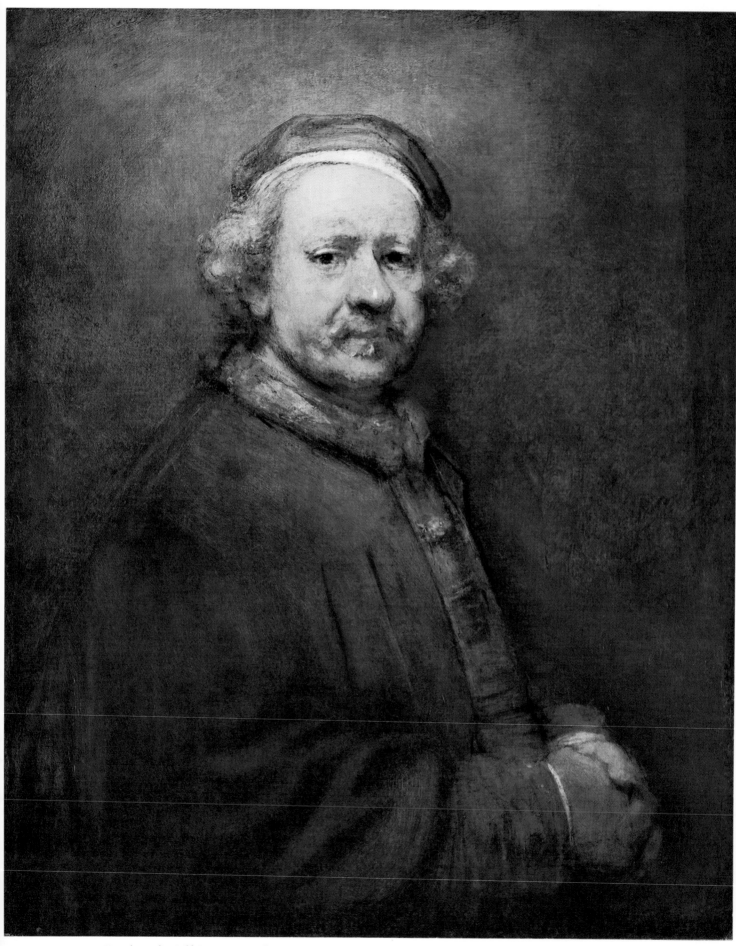

Rembrandt: Self-Portrait aged 63 (1669) 860 × 705 mm *The National Gallery, London* (page 125)

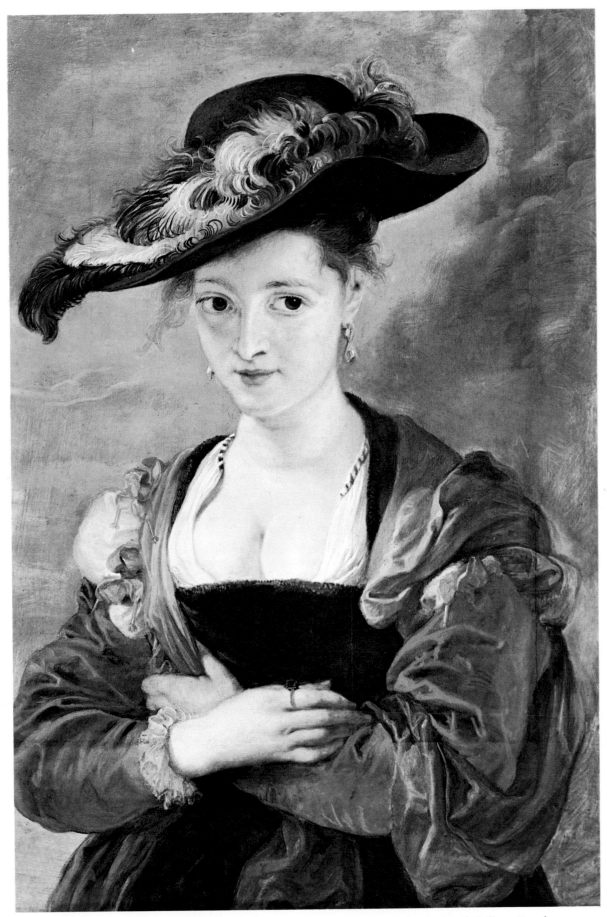

Rubens: Le Chapeau de Paille (*c* 1622–1625) 790 × 540/6 mm *The National Gallery, London*

The mixing of flesh colour always brings difficulties at the start. Practically every artist will advise with a different set of colours, a different recipe which will produce the illusive tones of flesh. The male skin tends to be a little stronger in tone and can be mixed from Indian red, yellow ochre and a trace of French ultramarine and, of course, white. The female flesh had better be mixed from cadmium yellow, cadmium red and a little French ultramarine and white.

Portrait painting has taken up the attention of painters of all schools and times. Much can be learnt by observation from successes of the past. What more dignified portrait of advancing age could there be than *Portrait of the Doge Loredan* by Giovanni Bellini. Note the gentle sensitivity of the handling of the face itself, the subtle contrast of the richly brocaded garment and the ingenious use of the cool blue-grey background. Giovanni Bellini (1428–1516) belonged to the Venetian School and amongst his pupils numbered Giorgione

Titian: Portrait of a Man
812 × 663 mm
*The National Gallery,
London*

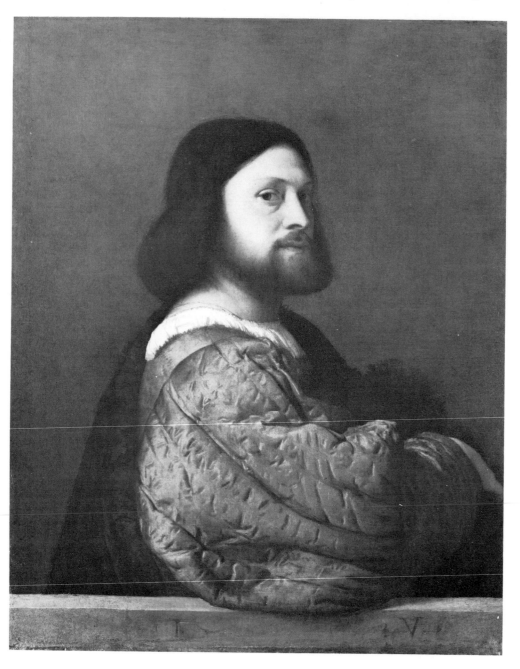

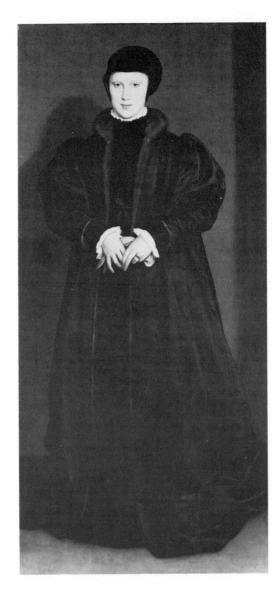

Hans Holbein the Younger: Christina
of Denmark, Duchess of Milan
(*c.* 1538) 1991 × 826 mm
The National Gallery, London

and Titian. Titian (1477–1576) himself was one of the great colourists whose
work could encompass on one hand the colourful paean to pagan idolatory
Bacchus and Ariadne and on the other the dignified *Portrait of a Man* (both in
the National Gallery). One of the most fascinating features is the way he has
made the perfectly painted large sleeve in the latter the focus of the composition.
It is obviously deliberate and underlines Titian's concern with representing the
third dimension. The delineation of the face has great strength and there is
considerable subtlety in the handling of the expression in the eyes.

Hans Holbein the Younger (1497–1543) with his *Duchess of Milan* displays
a carefully calculated restraint. This painting has recently been cleaned and
overpaints removed to show that Holbein's original background was of a
lighter tone and that he did have a shadow. One of the most consistent painters
of *self-portraits* was Rembrandt (1606–1669). Rembrandt had so many qualities
of greatness as a painter, it is difficult to pinpoint his most important. But perhaps it was his underlying humanity, his sensing of man's struggle that allowed
him to penetrate so deeply into his own character and that of many of his
sitters.

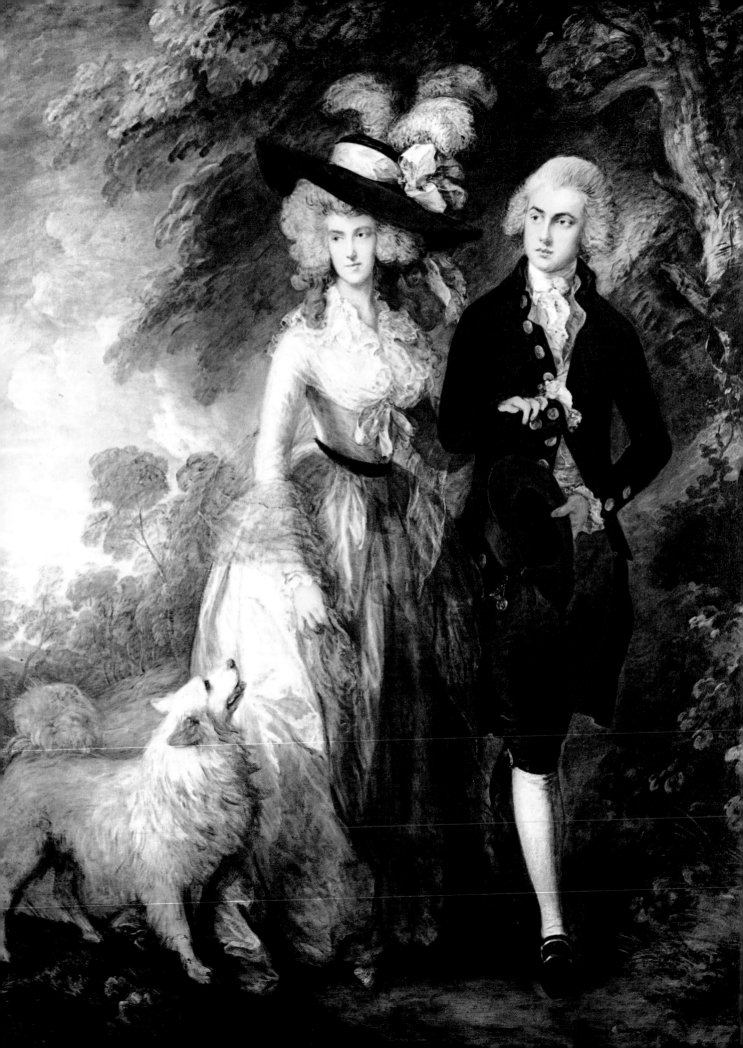

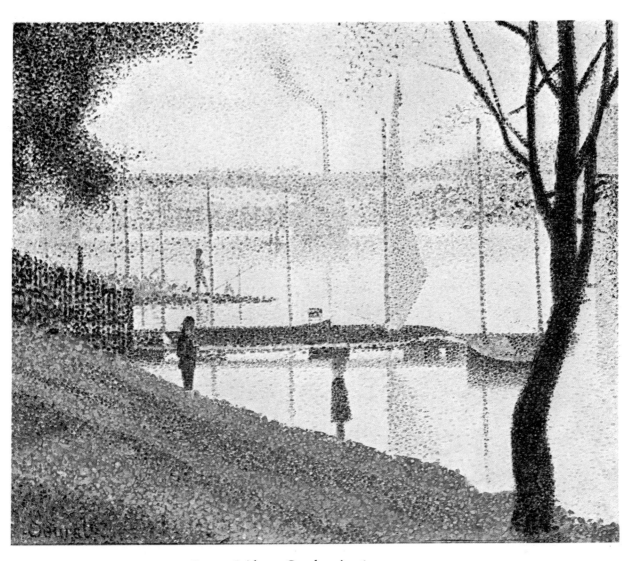

Seurat: Bridge at Courbevoie 460 × 550 mm
Courtauld Institute Galleries, London (page 142)

Opposite. **Gainsborough: The Morning Walk** (1785) 2361 × 1791 mm
The National Gallery, London (page 128)

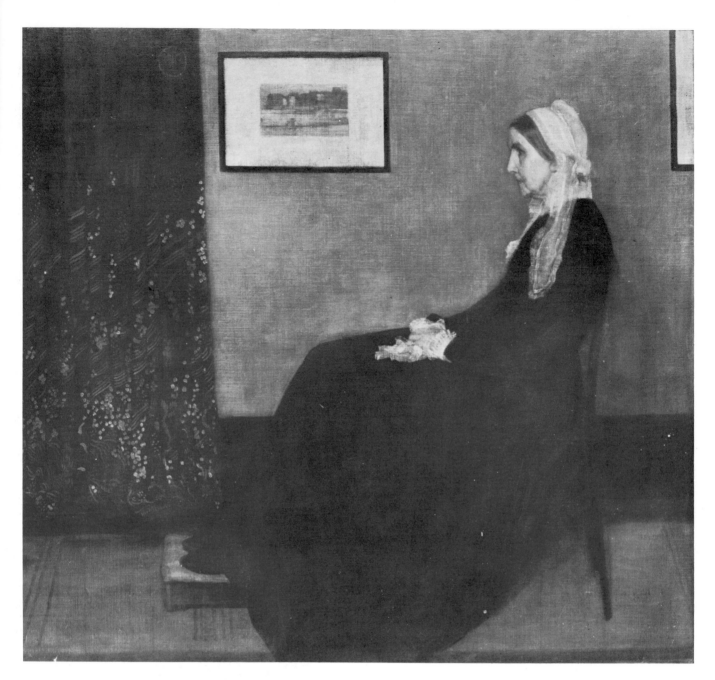

In the eighteenth century England produced many fine portrait painters. William Hogarth (1697–1764) with *The Shrimp Girl* (National Gallery) provides a glimpse of broad impressionism which must have shaken his contemporaries. Half close the eyes and look at this portrait and it can be seen how closely Hogarth kept to the principle of establishing the masses first. Perhaps the elegance of the Georgian times, the fashionable atmosphere of London and Bath, the rich fine ladies and gentlemen were best captured by Gainsborough (1727–1788). Apart from portraits he was also a master of landscape and his colour harmonies are immaculate. There is a quiet restraint of understatement.

In the latter part of the nineteenth century a number of refined aesthetic portraits were painted by James McNeill Whistler (1834–1903). He was from Lowell, Massachusetts, and studied with Gleyre in Paris. Whistler had a highly personal genius. His colour sense was delicate and his posing original, very different from the virility of Augustus John, a bohemian, flamboyant personality who seldom completely finished a picture. John had brush-work that was full of the best qualities of the painter as in *The Orange Jacket*, Tate Gallery. He had the ability to arrest motion and pin down the characters of his sitters.

One final glance at an approach to the portrait. Graham Sutherland in his conception of *Somerset Maugham* is combining tremendous technical ability with a psychological insight into his sitter's character, with perhaps just a touch of caricature.

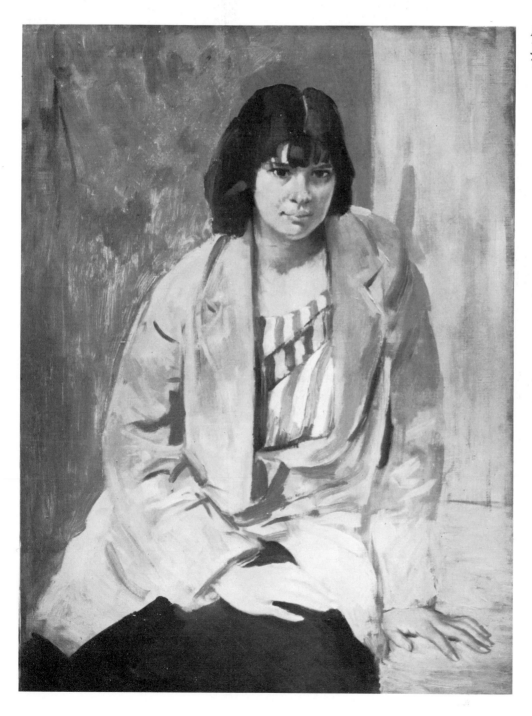

Augustus John: The Orange Jacket 1006 × 756 mm
Tate Gallery, London

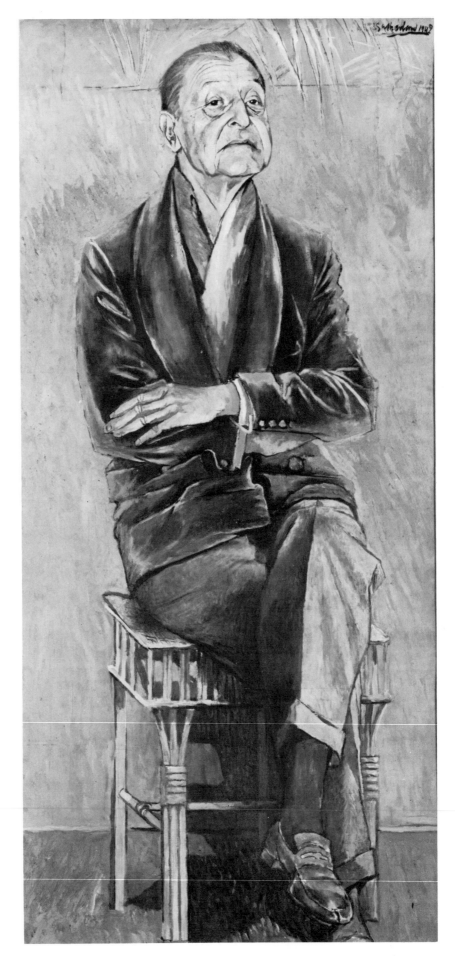

Miscellany

The studio

It may not always be possible to acquire a special room that will have all the refinements of the complete studio, but much can be done to make the best of what is available. Undoubtly the most important single thing is the light source. Ideally this should be from the north, as this will allow for a more even illumination, and be free at all times of the day from the direct rays of the sun. If this is not possible, a studio room with an east or a west window is second best, provided the limitations of difficulties in the early morning or the evening are accepted. A south window wherever possible should be ruled out, as it means for a large part of the day the sunlight will be beating in, bringing with it harsh glare and shadows that will make the correct judging of colours and tones almost impossible. If the studio is low down in a tall building and surrounded by other tall buildings, a large mirror mounted in metal brackets outside the window, and carefully angled, can greatly increase the amount of light coming in.

The problem of artificial light has been solved to some extent by the introduction of fluorescent tubes. These can be obtained in many different shades. Those that are known as 'warm-white' will generally give the most accurate colour registration. They are best mounted just over the top of the window, so that the light will come at the same angle as daylight.

The colour of the walls is important. Some painters today like to work in an all-white studio. But for many this may be too bright. Broadly speaking, a soft warm neutral grey is the best answer, as this will not conflict with the colours on the palette. It is not always easy to buy distemper or emulsion ready-made in this tint; therefore it is better to be able to mix the right colour. This can be done by adding small quantities of red, yellow and blue powder colours to white distemper or emulsion.

If the floor is timber and the boards are in good condition, it does not need more than a coat of stain and an occasional wax polish. It is inadvisable to have rubber or plastic tiles, as they can be seriously affected if turpentine substitute, paint remover and other liquids of such a nature are dropped on them. In fact, turpentine substitute will go through some plastic tiles in about an hour.

Space is one of the essentials in a studio because if a fairly large-sized picture is being painted it must be possible to step back several paces to judge properly the progress of the work. One method of economising with space is either to have built for you, or yourself make a painting table that has a series of drawers. The top of the table can have a sheet of plate glass cut to fit it which will serve as a palette. The first drawer may be divided into compartments for the different colours; the next drawer down can have divisions for the different types of brush, and if the dividing sections are made at an angle upwards from the rear

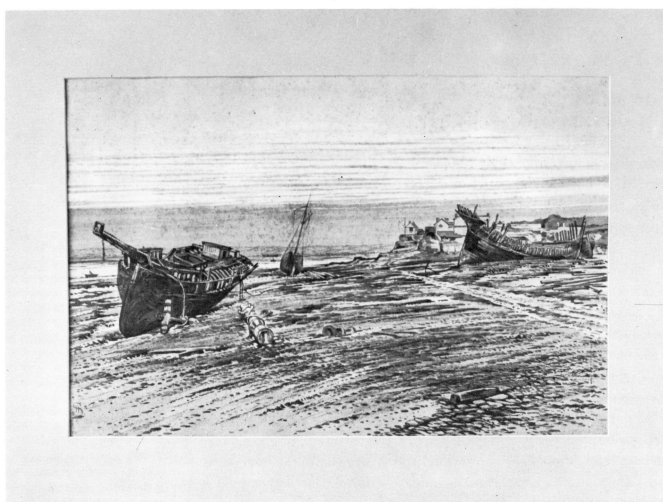

Above. When mounting a watercolour, a pastel or other type or drawing or print, make the sides and top of the mount equal and give a slightly greater width to the bottom.

Right. To cut a mount a very sharp blade is essential. If available a steel rule should be used and this can be clamped into position to release both hands. The mounting card should be laid on several layers of newspaper and the blade held to give an angled cut.

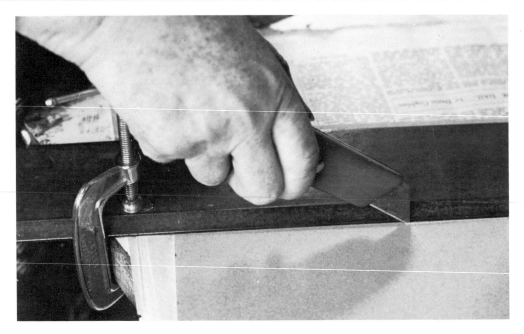

it will protect the bristles and the hairs of the brushes. Depending upon the height of the painting table, other drawers can be added for varnishes, mediums, solvents, painting knives, rags, etc. If the table is set on large castors it can be moved easily around the studio.

Easels were mentioned in the chapter on oil painting, but there is one other item which can be very useful in a studio and that is what is called a 'donkey'. It is really a short bench on which the artist sits astride on one end and the other end has a support on which to lean a drawing-board.

Framing

A painting without a frame or a proper mount always looks rather undressed and certainly cannot give of its best. There are principally two types of frame: one has a thin moulding and is incorporated with a mount, this is generally used for watercolours, drawings or prints; the other frame has a much thicker and wider moulding, has no mount, and is used for oils, tempera or acrylic when put on thickly.

The moulding for a watercolour should generally not be more than about an inch (25 mm) wide, and it can be purchased from an art shop or a timber dealer fairly cheaply. As the frame will need strength, some wood such as oak should be chosen. The corners of the frame will have to be cut exactly at 45 degrees. To do this, a mitre-block will be needed. If frame-making is going to be regularly done it is worth spending the money to buy a mitre-clamp that will not only hold firmly the piece of moulding being cut but will also include a guide which will hold the saw accurately in place. The corners should be joined with a good strong glue and one or two panel pins. An alternative to the panel pins is to cut out a groove across the mitre into which a slip of hardwood can be stuck and trimmed off. This will make the safest join.

Below left. When fixing a drawing to a mount, never stick it straight to the mount. Use strips of preferably a weaker paper and a light water-soluble paste or glue.

Below right. When fixing the backing to a frame with panel pins or small nails, always have an adequate support to hammer against to prevent damage to the corners of the frame.

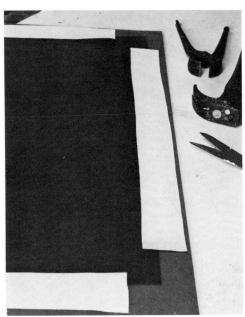

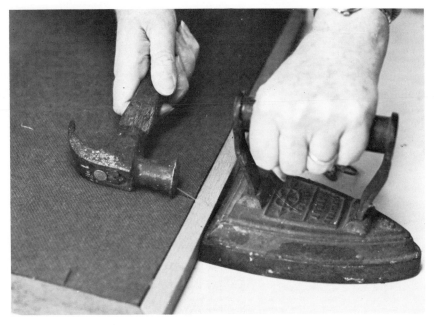

Frame finishing. *Top left.*
Plain wooden moulding
frames can be enhanced by
treating them with gesso.
This can be made with
whiting or marble dust and
mixed to a stiff consistency
with diluted rabbit skin glue.
The glue should first be
heated in a double saucepan
and then the powder added.
It should be applied hot. It
can be brushed on smooth or
with a stippled effect as here.

Top right. An alternative
finish can be made by
combing whilst the gesso is
still warm.

Bottom left. When the gesso
has hardened rough parts
can be scraped away or
sand-papered. Then to
provide an under colour to
enrich the gilding a coat of
Burnt Sienna should be
given. This should be
water-based.

Bottom right. When the
under colour has dried out a
gilding preparation can be
put on. This may be either a
liquid or a paste and can be
rubbed in with fingers and
thumbs to give a 'broken'
appearance. Finally a coat of
'porridge'-coloured distemper
can be added. This is then
wiped to bring through the
gild and so give an antique
look. If desired, a number of
other distemper tints can be
added to suit the picture,
and a coat of wax polish can
be given to fix the finish.

The mount for a watercolour or a gouache should be made from a good quality thick card. Cheap strawboard or cardboards should not be used as they are easily affected by damp and encourage mould growths which could attack the pictures. The aperture for the window in the mount should be, as a general guide, slightly above centre; for example, the width of mount at the sides and the top could be 2½″ (65 mm) and the width at the bottom 2¾″ (70 mm). Good quality thick mounting cards can be obtained with tinted face surfaces and they are so produced that when the bevelled cut for the window is made it shows white.

The cutting of a mount needs some practice and a strong wrist. Special mount cutting knives can be bought but most sharp-pointed modelling knives will do the job. The cut should be made using a steel ruler and with the blade held so that it will produce a bevelled edge of about 45 degrees in the mount. If desired, this kind of mount can be finished with a series of ruled lines or wash borders round the window.

As an alternative, after the window has been cut, cover the mount with either coloured and textured paper or with a textile. The easiest way to do this is to lay the piece of material that is to cover the mount flat on a table and then brush an adhesive over the face of the mount, pressing it firmly down on to the covering material. When the adhesive has hardened, diagonal cuts should be made through the covering material showing through the window. The flaps so formed should be drawn tightly through to the back of the mount and firmly stuck down. The painting should not itself be stuck to the mount but it should be fixed into position with four strips of paper or 'guards'. If the paper on which the picture has been painted is thin, it may be very slightly moistened from the back so that as it dries out it will tighten and remain flat.

The backing for a watercolour or drawing in its frame should be of hardboard. Never use three-ply wood as it is a great favourite with woodworm. The backing should be fixed into place using small panel pins; the hammering done against a heavy weight to prevent straining the frame.

Wide mouldings for oils or acrylics can be bought from the timber yard, but examples of mouldings three or four inches (75 or 100 mm) wide can be expensive. With a little thought and some rough work in a sketchbook it is possible to cut the price in half or even more. Architrave, picture-rail and glazing-bar mouldings can be fixed to lengths of 2″ (50 mm) × 1″ (25 mm) deal, and can produce a variety of serviceable mouldings. The cutting of the frame can be done in the same way as that for watercolours, only this time the mitred joints will need more secure fastening: a 2½″ (65 mm) nail or a combination of the inset slip of hardwood and a small triangular brass plate at each corner on the back of the frame.

The treatment of the frame will depend largely on the subject of the picture. The following process can be taken as a general guide and can be varied to suit individual cases. A rough gesso can be made up to this recipe: 1 ounce (30 g) of Scotch glue dissolved in a pint (6 dl) of water which is heated to about 85°C

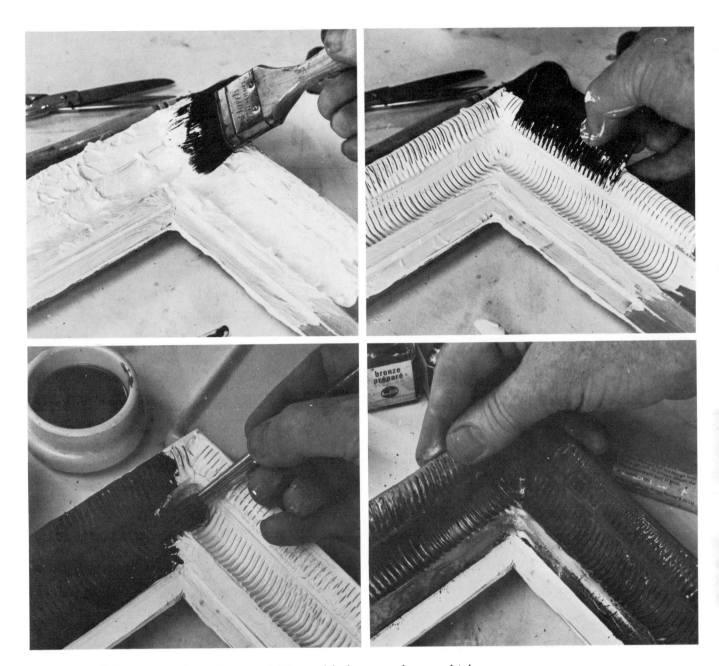

(187°F) and then enough ordinary whiting added to produce a thick cream. While the gesso is still hot it should be brushed on to the frame. This may be with a smooth finish or parts may be given a texture by stippling with the brush or combing in a regular or random manner. After twenty-four hours when the gesso has hardened, it may be desirable to smooth certain parts of the moulding with sandpaper.

The next step is to apply gilding, if it is wanted, and top finish. First of all, isolate the gesso with a saturated solution of shellac in methylated spirits. When this has dried the gild can be applied; this may be bronze powder mixed with cellulose or with acrylic medium or size. The gild may be brushed over-all or, if a semi-antique finish is required, it can be brushed on in a broken manner. Another way of giving a more gentle gilded effect is to use a product called Treasure Gold. This can be applied with a piece of cotton wool, rag or a finger tip. If it is desired to further enrich the gilding, a layer of Indian red oil colour diluted with turpentine can be put on before the gold. Once the gilding has been finished, to accentuate the antique or broken effect a few broad brush-strokes of weak green, grey-blue, cool red, and umber can be applied in a haphazard manner to the frame.

The final coat is prepared by mixing up some good quality distemper to a thin cream consistency; the colour of the distemper should be a warm yellow-grey. This is then brushed over the whole frame and allowed to dry. Then with a piece of moistened cotton wool small areas here and there can be wiped to expose, in the manner of a scumble, the undercoats of colour and gild. The frame may then be left mat or may be given a slight sheen by a light polish with some wax.

A canvas or a panel should never be nailed immovably into a frame. If this is done the concussion of the nailing may damage the picture and also natural movement of the wood or panel will be impossible. The picture should be fixed in either with small metal plates screwed to the frame and overlapping the picture or with some form of spring clip.

The screw eyes or hanging devices should be so fixed to the back of a frame that they allow the picture to hang with a slight forward tilt. If they are placed about a third of the way down, this will produce the result. The idea of tilting the picture is that it can be seen more easily and it also prevents much of the dust in the air from settling on the paint surface.

Picture care

Many pictures are sadly damaged each year because their cords or wires break and they fall from the wall. It is important at least once a year to inspect the hanging material as it can perish or rot quite quickly, particularly in damp climates.

Unglazed paintings unfortunately do gather dirt. Oil paintings certainly look much better without glass and although a varnish may give some protection it will in the end itself gather grime.

There are some horrific recipes for cleaning still in use. Household vegetables that include onions and potatoes are cut in half and wiped across the surface of a hapless painting. Some 'specialists' will advocate the use of new warm bread rubbed over the face of the painting, and there are plenty who believe in soap and water. One has only to consider what a painting is made of to see where the danger lies with these methods. An oil painting is an elaborate sandwich of size, canvas, priming, colours and varnish. If vegetable juices or moisture from the bread or soap and water get in amongst these layers, disaster is on the way. The size can swell and cause the paint to blister and flake away; mould growths can start on the back of the canvas or in cracks in the paint; the varnish can bloom.

The answer for the tyro picture-cleaner is '*don't*'. Picture cleaning is a com-

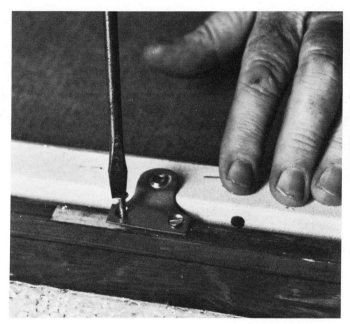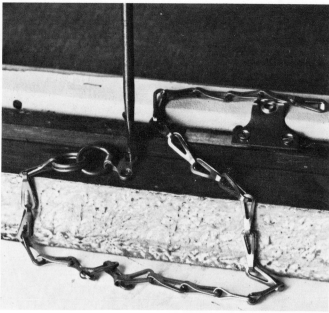

plicated and dangerous business and even if weak solvents for the varnish are used, it can be a very simple matter to cause paint loss. A gentle surface clean, however, is possible if it is done with observation and care. The mildest form is to gently wipe over the surface of the picture with pieces of cotton wool slightly moistened with turpentine substitute, the swabs should come away faintly grey as they lift the usual household dust. A more effective cleaning of the surface can be given by using Winton Picture Cleaner. The bottle containing the cleaner should be well shaken, and the cleaner sparingly applied to a small square of the area at a time. The swabs of cotton wool should be closely examined at each step to make sure no colour is being lifted. After the cleaning, the areas should be thoroughly wiped with pieces of cotton wool well moistened with turpentine substitute. When the whole picture has been treated and has dried out it should be re-varnished. It is stressed that neither of the cleaning methods above should be used unless the oil painting is at least five years old.

Good quality acrylic paint should produce a waterproof paint surface; therefore when it becomes dirty a picture carried out with acrylics can be gently washed with cold water applied with pieces of cotton wool. If the grime is obstinate it should be safe to use a little pure household soap or soft soap. This should be well rinsed off afterwards and the surface dried with clean soft rag. A preliminary test on the very edge of the picture which is hidden by the frame would be a safety measure.

Watercolours and gouaches should really always be kept under glass, as their cleaning is a very delicate process. In very damp climates they should be inspected regularly for 'foxing'. These small orange-brown spots that appear are a form of mould or bacteriological activity. They can be bleached out with a 5 per cent solution of hydrogen peroxide put on with a small paintbrush. As the stain disappears it should be mopped with clean white blotting paper and then several applications of distilled water should be made to remove the hydrogen peroxide, and these should also be blotted.

Left. When fixing a picture into a frame it is better to use small metal plates such as shelf-ears similar to the one being screwed down here. Hammering in nails tends to damage frames, and also the painting.

Right. The place where the ring should be fixed which is to take the hanging chain or cord should be about one third of the way down from the top of the frame. This will allow the frame and picture to hang forward with a slight tilt which makes the painting easier to see and also to a large extent prevents dust falling on to the surface of an unglazed picture.

Glossary of terms

Action Painting A term that is applied to a method of painting that was first evolved in America in 1947 by Jackson Pollock. The theory is that the unconscious mind of the painter will affect the picture as it is painted. The colour can be sprinkled, splashed and sprayed on and whilst wet can be manipulated with brushes, knives, rollers, etc. Action painting must not be confused with true Abstract Art, which is often a carefully organised method.

Aerograph Colours These are specially prepared to be used with colour sprays and are normally extra finely ground, so that they will pass through the fine nozzle.

Agate Burnishers For re-surfacing paper after scraping out a mistake with a knife or for burnishing gold leaf.

Alla Prima This is a term which is primarily applicable to oils. It means that the picture is completed in one sitting whilst all the paint is wet, and thus there is only one layer of colour to dry out and this should not then be liable to crack.

Amadou A brown soft dried fungus which can be used to remove mistakes in preliminary charcoal drawing.

Art Cleaner A soft erasing material which will not only remove pencil and charcoal but also will clean off dirt, grease and perspiration from paper, card, canvas and panels. It has the advantage that it is unlikely to damage the texture of the surface.

Asymmetry With this form of composition the main masses are not grouped in a central, balanced manner; they tend to be to one side or the other.

Bloom A light misty cloud that can appear on the surface of natural resin varnishes. It is very often caused either by the varnish being applied on a damp day or by the picture being continuously exposed to a cold damp atmosphere.

Body Colour A term to describe the use of opaque white with pure watercolour.

Bole A thin layer of warm-coloured earth which is laid over gesso before laying gold leaf. This is to provide an enriching effect for the very thin metal.

Broken Colour A method of applying the colour with small strokes of different tints and tones laid alongside each other, so that from a few yards away the whole appears to merge together.

Camera Lucida An instrument for copying, enlarging or reducing drawings.

Camera Obscura An apparatus for projecting on to paper or canvas an image of an object.

Canvas Pins Small round wooden blocks with points each side for carrying two wet canvases face to face; one canvas pin is put in each corner.

Cartoon Actual-size drawings on thin paper that are prepared for large mural works. The principal lines of the cartoon are then pricked through using a roulette, which is a small wheel with sharp cog-like spikes. The cartoon is then temporarily fixed against the wall on which the mural is to be painted and the lines are 'pounced'. 'Pouncing' is done by putting some powdered graphite into three or four layers of muslin, folding it into a small bag and dabbing along the lines. Some of the graphite will come through the muslin.

Casein Colours With these, the pigments are mixed with casein, an extract from milk, and the colours will handle in a similar manner to true egg tempera, although they will not be so permanent or elastic. Casein colours can be used for gouache with fairly heavy impasto. When they are dry they are best left unvarnished or unwaxed as either of these treatments can alter many of the colours.

Chiaroscuro The handling, arrangement and control of light and shade in a painting. It is worth studying the work of Caravaggio and Rembrandt, as both these masters had a deep understanding of the method.

Classic Art With this the artist goes back to the disciplines and the manner of the Greeks for his basic ideas. It is in complete opposition to the freedom of the later romantics.

Cleaning In its general sense, this means the removal of surface dirt from a picture, but applied to oil paintings it means the removal of the old darkened layers of varnish. It is a process that should not be embarked upon lightly, as it is very easy to remove not only the dirt but also the paint itself.

Composition The arrangement of the main masses and details in a picture so that they produce harmony and agreement.

Copal Oil Medium One of the more common liquid additives for oil colours. The medium will tend to enrich and gloss the paint film and also increase the drying speed.

Coquille Board This is a recently introduced surface or support which can be used for watercolour or gouache. It has an interesting texture built up of arrangements of small dots.

Diminishing Glass A form of reverse magnifying glass that can reduce a picture, so that an idea of its size if it is to be reproduced smaller can be seen.

Diptych and Triptych Pictures consisting of two or three hinged panels. The terms generally refer to altarpieces.

Distemper Colours These can be purchased from a decorator or ironmonger. The colours will not have great tinting power and should not be used for permanent work. They may even have dyes mixed with them.

Encaustic It implies the use of pigments mixed with wax. It may be done in one of two ways: the surface of the support can be treated with wax and then the colours are placed on to the wax and sealed in by the use of a hot iron; the other method is to use a heated palette, the colours are mixed on the palette into the molten wax and are then applied to the support with brushes, painting knives or small droppers; finally the whole is fused together with the hot iron.

Filler Inert additives that are sometimes mixed with powerful pigments to reduce their strength.

Fresco A painting on a plaster wall. The technique may be either buon fresco or fresco secco. In buon fresco the painting is carried out straight on to a freshly plastered wall whilst the plaster is still wet. In fresco secco the plaster wall is allowed to dry out thoroughly first and then the hard plaster is soaked with lime water before painting begins. Of the two, buon fresco is the more permanent, as the colours soak in.

Fugitive Pigments Colours which may fade or darken, or react with other pigments to change or destroy them.

Glaze The laying of a thin coat of transparent colour over another colour.

Gouache Watercolour painting carried out in an opaque manner. The colour can be applied either with hair or bristle brushes and with light impasto.

Grisaille A picture painted in a grey monochrome.

Impasto The ridges of paint raised by the brush or painting knife.

Imprimatura A thin wash of colour put over the priming before painting the picture. It is generally of a warm brown tone: with oils it can be applied mixed with turpentine or turpentine substitute, and with acrylics it is mixed with acrylic medium and water.

Isolate To apply a substance such as latex, shellac or size that will prevent the penetration of watercolour or oils.

Lay Figure A fully-jointed wooden or plastic figure that is used by the painter for copying poses. The figure may be quite small or life-size.

Licence Freedom for the artist to rearrange objects and parts of the scene to suit his imagination and taste.

Mahlstick A long thin stick with a padded knob at one end held by a painter to rest his brush hand on when painting fine details.

Marouflage To mount a canvas or paper on to a hardboard or wooden panel with an adhesive.

Medium This term has two meanings in art. The first describes the method or material in which the artist works. (Here 'media' has been used for the plural.) The second is the name for liquid additives for acrylics, watercolour or oils. (Here 'mediums' has been used for the plural.)

Monochrome A picture painted in varying tones of one colour.

Mural A painting on a wall carried out in fresco, oil, tempera or other media.

Ox Gall An additive to assist the adhesion of watercolour or gouache to shiny surfaces.

Pantograph An instrument for enlarging, reducing or copying a picture to the same size.

Pastiche A picture that consists largely of fragments lifted or borrowed from the work of other artists.

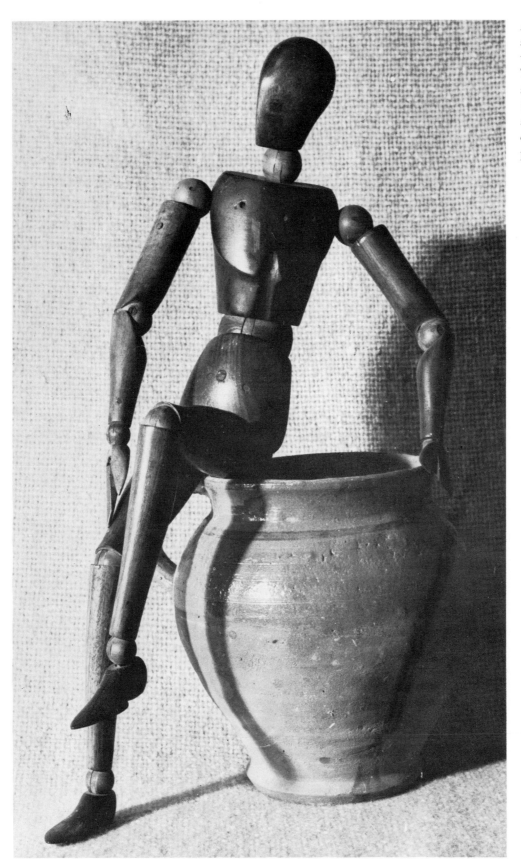

A lay figure can be of great assistance when working with conversation pieces. The example shown here is about eighteen inches (46 cm) high. The limbs are all fully jointed and will only go into positions possible to the human body.

Palette The first meaning implies the surface on which the artist mixes his colours. The second is the choice of colours he uses.

Pentimento (pl. pentimenti) The ghostly image that can appear in the top layer of paint, showing previous versions that have not been removed.

Perspective A mathematical law that governs the lines and planes in a picture to produce the impression of depth.

Pointillism The application of primary and pure colours in small dots close together, so that when viewed from a few yards away the eye does the mixing; for example, to get green, small dots of blue and yellow are placed beside each other. It was developed by the French painter Seurat.

Priming The preparation of a canvas or panel for acrylic and oil painting.

Scumble To drag one colour in a broken manner over another colour or to soften a line or a stroke of colour by rubbing with the finger.

Sgraffito A method of cutting through from one layer to expose an under-layer or several layers, which can be adapted to any medium. With watercolour it may be done using a razor blade, a sharp knife or sandpaper. With oil or acrylics the pointed end of a brush handle or any suitable sharp instrument can be used.

Siccatif A medium for oil painting containing linseed oil, natural resins and turpentine, which will greatly speed up the rate of drying. However, it should be used with care, as it can cause some colours to crack quite severely.

Stipple To paint with the brush held more or less at right angles to the support and laying the colour as small spots or tiny strokes.

Stretcher The wooden frame which stretches the canvas. It has specially mitred corners into which wedges can be driven to slightly expand the size of the frame.

Support The name for any material which provides the surface on which a painting is carried out.

Symmetry The opposite of asymmetry. The placing of the main masses and objects in a composition so that they are equal on both sides.

Tempera A group name for variations of emulsion or watercolour opaque methods. It implies that the pigments may be mixed with egg white, egg yolk, glue or casein. True egg tempera, which is one of the most permanent methods of painting, means that the pigments are mixed only with pure egg yolk and perhaps a trace of some disinfectant.

Trompe l'Oeil A picture that has great technical skill in the portrayal of natural objects to such a degree that the eye may be deceived.

Vehicle The substance which binds the colours; for example, acrylic medium with acrylics; linseed oil with oils; egg yolk with tempera; gum with water-colour; etc.

Index

Acknowledgements

The illustration at the top of page 80 is reproduced by gracious permission of Her Majesty the Queen.
The illustration on page 51 is reproduced by permission of the Board of Trinity College, Dublin.

Photographs
Alinari, Florence 81; Bayerische Staatsgemäldesammlungen, Munich 108; British Museum 13, 85; Camera and Pen International, London 120 bottom left; Courtauld Institute Galleries, London 98; Photographie Giraudon, Paris 120 top right, 128; Hallwylska Museet, Stockholm 88; Hamlyn Group – J. R. Freeman 76, 77 top, 80 bottom; Hamlyn Group – Graham Portlock 55 bottom, 78 top, 78 bottom, 97; Hamlyn Group – John Webb 55 top, 82, 87, 94, 95, 106, 110, 111, 114, 115, 123; Hamlyn Group Picture Library 50, 51, 62, 63, 107, 119, 127; Mansell Collection, London 79 top; Mansell-Anderson 89; Bildarchiv foto Marburg 121 right; Metropolitan Museum of Art, New York 102; Museum of Fine Arts, Boston, Massachusetts 90, 91; Musée de l'Homme, Paris 9; Musées Nationaux, Paris 86, 99; National Gallery, London 54, 92, 93, 109, 112 top and bottom, 122, 124, 125, 126; National-museum, Stockholm 83; H. Roger-Viollet, Paris 11, 120 top left; Stichting Johan Maurits van Nassau, The Hague 103; Tate Gallery, London 113, 116 top, 116 bottom, 117, 120 bottom right, 121 left, 129, 130; Victoria and Albert Museum, London 77 bottom, 79 bottom; Yale University Art Gallery, New Haven, Connecticut 118.